Landfall Walks

Bob A~~cton~~

AROUND
PADSTOW

Circular Walks
from Porthcothan
to Wadebridge and Bodmin

First published 1991
Revised edition, 1995

LANDFALL PUBLICATIONS
Landfall, Penpol, Devoran, Truro, Cornwall TR3 6NW

Copyright © R. S. Acton 1995

A CIP catalogue record for this book is available
from the British Library.

ISBN 1 873443 19 6

Typesetting, maps and drawings by Bob Acton

Printed by the Troutbeck Press
and bound by R. Booth Ltd., Antron Hill, Mabe, Penryn, Cornwall

NOTE TO THE SECOND EDITION

Nearly four years have passed since *Around Padstow* was first published,
and in that time a good many changes have occurred which necessitated
revisions to the text or maps or both. The most dramatic of these changes is
the building, at long last, of the Wadebridge Bypass. This has had a
particular impact on Walk 5, the full version of which now unfortunately
involves walking across the new road at a point where there ought to be a
footbridge, an underpass or at least a central island. Many other small
changes to the descriptions and directions - affecting mainly Walks 1, 5 and
6 - have been made as a result of reports from users of the book or
information provided by local farmers and landowners. Mr Anthony
Hawkey of the Ramblers' Association has again helped with revisions, and
keeps me abreast of footpath developments whenever we meet at concerts at
St Endellion. I am most grateful for the help of all these people, and hope
that any problems which arise in connection with this new edition will also
be drawn to my attention.
Probably the most noticeable innovation in the new book, apart from the
cover, is the addition of an extra walk. Rock is so easily reached by ferry
from Padstow, and St Enodoc Church is so celebrated, that I could not resist
breaking my self-imposed rule of limiting my territory to the south-western
side of the Camel estuary. I was tempted to make the further addition of the
wonderful walk around Pentire Point and the Rumps, but finally decided
against that in view of the existence of a cheap and excellent National Trust
leaflet detailing routes around that headland.

Bob Acton - January 1995

CONTENTS

Introduction and Acknowledgements 4

Walk 1: St Merryn, Treyarnon and Porthcothan *(About 6 miles)* 5

Walk 2: Treyarnon, Harlyn Bay and Trevose Head *(Nearly 7 miles,
with two shorter options)* 12

Walk 3: Padstow, Trevone and Stepper Point *(Just over 7 miles)* 19

Walk 4: Lower Halwyn, Padstow, Little Petherick and St Issey
(About 7 miles, including a diversion into Padstow) 25

Walk 5: Wadebridge, Tregunna and St Breock *(About 5 miles; can
be shortened to 3 miles or lengthened to 7.)* 33

Walk 6: Wadebridge, Polbrock and Burlawn *(About 6 miles)* 42

Walk 7: Polbrock, Dunmere and Nanstallon *(About 6 miles, plus
just over a mile if Ruthernbridge is included)* 46

Walk 8: St Breock Beacon, Tregustick and Trewithian *(About 5 miles)* . . 52

Walk 9: Withiel and St Wenn *(About 4.5 miles, or about 6 miles
if you include a diversion to Demelza)* 56

Walk 10: Withiel, the Tremore valley and Ruthernbridge *(Nearly 5
miles; about 3 miles if Ruthernbridge is left out.)* 62

Walk 11: Rock and St Enodoc Church *(About 3 miles)* 67

Sunday Afternoon Specials: Shorter Circular Walks 71

Notes on the Camel Trail and the Saints' Way 72

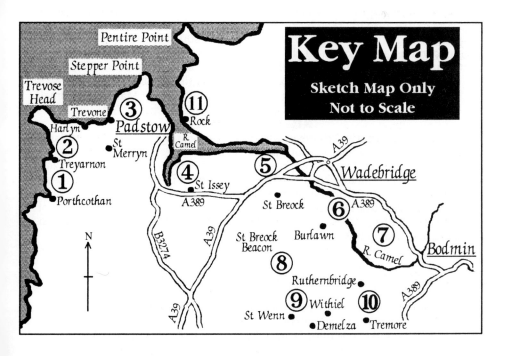

INTRODUCTION

Every book of walks I have written so far has left me wondering at the amazing variety of landscapes Cornwall has to offer within each small region. Researching this book has taken my wife and me to towering cliffs, wide-spreading "towans" or dunes, packed holiday beaches, thickly wooded valleys, windswept moorland, estuary waters ploughed by noisy speedboats, estuary mudflats dotted with a few placid wading birds..... In fact, I don't think it would be too difficult to devise a perfectly manageable walk that would include all of those, with extra contrast added in the form of a stream of fast traffic on the Wadebridge bypass and a country road less than a mile away where you feel the intrusion of one car would be a topic of local conversation for years. Padstow is a particularly good base for a walking holiday because three long and fully waymarked footpaths meet there (see page 72 for notes on two of them; the third is the South West Way, alias the coast path), and each has its own unique character. My hope is that this little book will help those who are visiting the area to discover some of its special beauties and a little of its history, and even perhaps encourage those who have lived here for many years to put on a stout pair of shoes and remind themselves how lucky they are.

USING THE BOOK

The introductory boxed notes are designed to be read before you set off: they include information about such matters as opening times of places you may wish to visit, and guidance about things you may need to wear or take with you - it would not be possible to get food or drink on some of the walks, for example. I recommend you to take on all the walks the relevant OS map, because my sketch maps don't have the kind of accurate detail you might need if you went astray. Landranger 200 (Newquay, Bodmin and surrounding area) covers all eleven walks; the Pathfinder series is even more useful for walkers, but you would need four of them (numbers 1337, 1338, 1346 and 1347), and the route of Walk 6 is actually divided among all four!

RIGHTS OF WAY

I have used "definitive" rights of way wherever possible, and in the few cases where there is any doubt about public rights of access I have tried to make the position clear. Please note, however, that the inclusion of a path, track or road on a recommended route in this book cannot in itself confer any rights of usage, and the ultimate responsibility for where you walk must be your own. If difficulties do arise, either through errors of mine or because of changes that have taken place since I researched the walks, I should be most grateful to hear about them.

ACKNOWLEDGEMENTS

As usual, I have received help from people too numerous to list here individually, but I must say a special thank-you to Anthony Hawkey, who checked through the complete text of the walks and made many useful suggestions and corrections, especially concerning rights of way.

WALK 1
COASTAL FOOTPATH ROUND WALK NO. 1
ST MERRYN, TREYARNON
AND PORTHCOTHAN

About six miles.

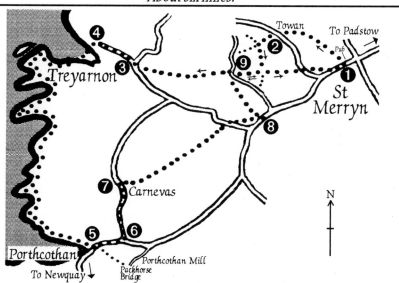

As well as a breathtakingly beautiful section of the coast path, this route includes very attractive inland walking among gently rolling hills and valleys. The countryside here is dotted with picturesque cottages and farm buildings, such as those at Towan, Trevear, Treyarnon, Carnevas and - if you go that way - Porthcothan Mill. Little road walking is involved. Although we did not encounter any great difficulties, not all the inland paths are well maintained: many of the stiles have very wet patches on one side or both during rainy spells, and on two occasions I have found fields ploughed and planted with no attempt to reinstate the path crossing them. This can hardly be called an easy walk, then, but your efforts will be richly rewarded, especially if you're lucky enough to go on a day like the one we chose the first time, in February, with bright sunshine but enough wind to ensure that the Atlantic breakers put on a spectacular show along this deeply indented stretch of coast. There is a shop at Porthcothan, and at the main crossroads in St Merryn, quite near the start of the walk, are several more. The walk as written starts and ends at the Farmers Arms, St Merryn, but the only practicable parking there is for pub customers, so in case you don't intend to be one I have suggested two other start-points where there are public car parks. In addition, there are two pubs along the way. The first is the Treyarnon Bay Hotel, which normally serves bar snacks but on Sundays (and we were there on a Sunday) does only a four-course lunch. Although this sounded like good value at £4, we doubted our ability to complete the walk after it. The atmosphere there was friendly, but we weren't too sure about the plastic Neptune, figureheads, diver and mermaid. At the far end of the coastal walk is the Tredrea Inn at Porthcothan, which has been highly rated for its restaurant food. Treyarnon and Porthcothan offer surfing and safer bathing than many other beaches along the north coast.

To drive to St Merryn (*) from Padstow, take the main coast road towards Newquay (B3276). Continue beyond the church, and after nearly half a mile you will reach the crossroads where the shops are. Just past that on your right you will see the Farmers Arms. There is parking opposite for customers. Alternatively there are car parks at Treyarnon Bay and Porthcothan, from which you could pick up the directions at point 4 or 5.

ST MERRYN

St Merryn Church is quite a long way from the route of this walk: I was unable to include it on an attractive round walk, despite the generous supply of paths leading to it according to the maps. Though not among Cornwall's most graceful churches as seen from the outside ("a plain, low, storm-resisting building", as Betjeman puts it), it is an ancient one and worth a visit, especially for the beautiful stone and font carved from the blue-grey "Cataclewse" or "Cataclewse" stone quarried from the headland west of Harlyn Bay. The font was brought from the ruined Chapel of St Constantine: see Walk 2. The Church is dedicated to St Marina. This name may be a corruption of Merin or Meren, a Celtic saint regarded as male in Wales and Brittany but female in Cornwall. Gender was very much at issue in the case of St Marina, too: she was smuggled into a monastery in Asia Minor by her father and lived all her life as a monk. Her male impersonation was so successful that she was accused and found guilty of fathering the child of an innkeeper's daughter! Five years' penance for this deed was apparently regarded as adequate for her to qualify as a saint.

1 The path starts on the same side of the road as the Farmers Arms, and just beyond it (if you have approached from the east). Walk with the hedge on your left at first; beyond the gate, the hedge is on your right. After a second gate, continue in the same direction, cutting off the right-hand corner of the field; head towards the group of houses. The first stile is in the right-hand corner, and the second is just to the left of attractive farm buildings at Towan. (The name means sand-hill; quite surprising, perhaps, because the dunes at Constantine Bay are at least a mile away; but Towan Farm is on the western side of the settlement, and presumably its land extends, or once extended, as far as the coast.)

2 At the road turn right, passing among more pretty buildings around Towan Farm, and take the signed public footpath on the left, over one stile and then another crossing what was once a small gate on the right. Now go diagonally across the field to a blue-painted stile near the corner. Next, turn left and follow the hedge on your left, through a gate at the first field boundary and over a stile across fencing at the second. At the third there is a gap. Here the path goes straight on, to be crossed by another at the centre of the field, where you need to turn right; this is just short of the electricity-supply pole. Now go through the gateway ahead and straight down the centre of the field; when roofs come into view, head towards the one furthest left. Cross the stile at the corner and continue in the same direction past Trevear Cottage. Ignore the public footpath sign immediately before the second cottage; continue for about another 50 yards and turn left at the footpath signed to Treyarnon Bay. After crossing the stile on the left of the metal gate, climb the slope to another stile, cross that and then go just slightly right of straight ahead, over two more stiles. Keeping near the top of the slope, continue ahead to a stile just left of the field corner, where you get your first sight of the sea. Next go slightly right, diagonally across the field to a wooden gate, then straight on along the obvious path towards farm buildings and the sea. The gate brings you to a road.

3 Turn right, and then follow the sign left to Treyarnon Bay, passing the stone buildings of Treyarnon Farm. Soon you reach the coast, with the Treyarnon Bay Hotel on your right.

4 Follow the acorn signs to the left, across the beach - where you have a stream to ford - and up steps on the far side. The coast path to Porthcothan cuts across the necks of most of the small headlands, but if you have a

Treyarnon Farm

Looking north towards Treyarnon.
Dinas Head and the Trevose lighthouse on the skyline.

reasonable head for heights it's well worth going out to them for the splendid views, especially if the sea is lively. Please be cautious, however, when approaching the cliff edges, because they are very unstable.

The large island just off the cliffs on the southern side of Treyarnon beach is a nature reserve, called Trethias, from a nearby farm. The three deepest coves within the first half-mile-or-so are called Pepper, Warren and Fox. The names are intriguing; "Pepper" could perhaps allude to a spicy cargo washed up there (compare "Pepper Hole", near Stepper Point), and the other two names may refer to the many caves, or of course they could be literal: I don't know if foxes are found in these parts, but Gilbert Garceau's little book about Porthcothan has some vivid paragraphs about the vast numbers of rabbits there were before myxomatosis struck.

The OS maps mark ancient settlements on or near most of the headlands; the two ramparts and ditches linking Pepper and Warren Coves are the clearest visible evidence of early man. The view ahead from Fox Cove to Minnows Islands is especially fine. Rounding the cove, you pass an ancient barrow (burial mound). On the south side of the same cove, look back to the rocks on the north side, where if the tide is right it is possible to make out the remains of a wrecked ship. According to Philip Carter's description of this area for the South West Way's series of booklets, this was a merchant vessel, previously a naval auxiliary, called the *Hemsley I*, which was driven ashore here in 1969. "Parts of her were salvaged," writes Mr Carter, "and the rough track on the cliff top is the remains of the road made and used for this purpose."

Just before the flight of well-made granite steps is a small waterfall. The close-up view of the Minnows is superb - a reminder of Bedruthan Steps, which lies just beyond Porthcothan. (See *Around Newquay*, Walk 1.) A magnificent piece of "herringbone" walling has been built at a point where cliff falls have been particularly serious. Close to this is another primitive barrow.... and then the path descends to the road behind the beach at Porthcothan (*).

PORTHCOTHAN

"Harbour of proclamations" is Oliver Padel's only suggestion for the name's meaning, which, as he says, "would make little sense". It is pronounced "P'thcothan", with the middle syllable said to rhyme with "broth". Gilbert Garceau's *Porthcothan, Past and Present* has a fascinating series of photographs comparing the village in 1985 with the same scenes 60 or more years earlier. Apart from the recent proliferation of houses, especially on the southern side of the bay, the most striking change is the almost total absence of trees in the old pictures: "At that time," (1925), writes Mr Garceau, "any old person spoken to would confirm that they remembered the whole of the valley cultivated down to the stream, hillside and all." Even the upper part of the beach, above tide level, was, he says, probably cultivated; the dunes in their present form were created during World War 2 when mines were laid on the beach, and the fences at the top, into which the marram grass grew, prevented sand from being blown in drifts across the road. Porthcothan Mill, fed by a long leat which starts where two streams join, about half a mile up the valley, apparently ceased working about 1914. In the valley above the mill are still traces of what Joan Rendell (in *North Cornwall in the Old Days*) describes as a "thousand yard long cave where the smugglers hid kegs of brandy and other goods brought in by their luggers." I have heard it said that this "cave" or tunnel originated as a fogou, but according to Craig Weatherhill's *Cornovia* all the Cornish fogous are west of the Fal estuary. Among the visitors to Porthcothan Mr Garceau mentions General Smuts, Lord Baden-Powell, R.A.Butler and D.H.Lawrence. Lawrence, it seems, outraged local opinion here, as also at Zennor, by leaving his house lights on despite World War 1 blackout regulations.

---

5 For the post office / store and the easiest way on to the beach, turn right. There are some good caves on the south side of the beach. To continue the walk, however, turn left (or, more accurately, go straight on up the hill) at the road. Be careful here, because this road can be busy in summer.

(After a few yards there is a footpath on the right, leading to Porthcothan Mill and the valley to Penrose. At the time of writing the first edition of this book, the footpath up the valley, shown as a right of way on the OS maps at least since 1960, was in dispute, and three years later things were no further

The pack–horse bridge near the mill at Porthcothan

forward. *If the matter is eventually resolved in favour of walkers, I would strongly recommend extending Walk 1 via Penrose, then Trevean and Kerketh farms, returning to the main road between Shop and Trehemborne. I haven't walked all of that myself, but I know the valley between Porthcothan and Penrose is a magical place, and the rest of the route appears to be intact and signposted. At Trevean there is a short stretch where there is no official right of way; I discussed this matter with the owners, and they are at present quite happy for walkers to use their drive, although of course they are entitled to withdraw their permission. Even if the valley to Penrose remains inaccessible, I suggest you make a short diversion across the marshy area at the seaward end of it, up to the former mill and the old packhorse bridge just beyond it, returning by the same path.)*

To continue the main walk, go on up the road.

6 Opposite the Tredrea Inn turn left on to a quieter road, continuing for about half a mile till you reach Carnevas, with its impressive but dilapidated stone buildings. (My OS maps give no hint of ancient remains here, but Oliver Padel explains the name as a combination of Cornish *cruc* , barrow, and *neved*, pagan sacred place, sacred grove.)

7 Turn right at the footpath sign just past Carnevas, following the main track beside the buildings, through a wooden gate, and then along to a stile beside a second gate. The right of way goes slightly left across the centre of the field, crosses a barbed-wire fence by means of a stile, and continues down to another stile. There are rough stepping stones both sides of it, and a piece of fencing (possibly a relic of one of the footbridges mentioned on the OS map) partly blocks it. Beyond that, go slightly right, under the electricity-supply lines, to another stile, then straight on, diagonally across a field where the path needed reinstating; head just right of the roofs of four houses to a stile near the field corner. Continue to another stile just right of the houses, and cross the road and the stile opposite. This path cuts off the corner of the field and reaches the road again opposite the oldest cottage. (In the summer of 1994 we had to fight our way through head-high sweetcorn to get there.) Be careful of the steps down to the road, which can be slippery - and traffic on the road tends to be fast.

8 Turn left, then immediately left again at the entrance to Trehemborne Farm. Keep left of the buildings, go through the small metal gate, and after the gravelled patch head downhill to the right towards the cottages at Trevear. After the footbridge, go through the small wooden gate beside the log store of the left-hand cottage and pass close to the cottage itself.

9 For a short distance now you are back on the route you came by. Turn right on the lane, and after the next cottage take the footpath signed on the left. Go up the centre of the field, through the gateway and ahead to the stile in the hedge. Cross this - and now you are on new ground again. Continue in the same line to a stile just left of a row of slate-hung houses, and cross the road. If the kissing gate ahead is still too overgrown to use, go through the gap on the left, and still go on in the same direction to a small gate on the left side of the tallest building, St Merryn Village Hall. Turn left on the road to return to the starting point.

FOR A VERY FINE WALK WESTWARDS FROM PORTHCOTHAN, INCLUDING BEDRUTHAN STEPS AND AN INLAND SECTION AROUND ST EVAL CHURCH, SEE *AROUND NEWQUAY*, NO. 5 IN THE LANDFALL SERIES.

CORRECTION: Point 8 in the directions
I have learnt that there is no public right of way through Trehemborne farmyard. Until and unless an alternative path acceptable to the landowner is created, walkers will need to continue along the road and take the first turning on the left, in order to pick up the suggested route again at point 9. See the sketch map on page 5.

WALK 2
COASTAL FOOTPATH ROUND WALK NO. 2
TREYARNON, HARLYN BAY
AND TREVOSE HEAD
Nearly seven miles.
Two shorter options are also described.

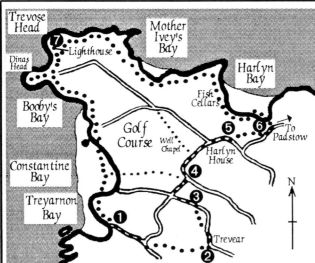

Most of the best beaches in the Padstow area are on this stretch of coast, so holiday and retirement bungalows, caravan sites and other legacies of an era when planning regulations seem to have had even less effect than they do today proliferate along much of it. A large area which was once noted for marsh flora and abundant wildlife is now a golf course, and in a famous quarry overlooking the sea now lurks a large sewage treatment plant. On the other hand, Trevose Head has impressive cliffs as well as a lighthouse you can visit, and the views from the west side of Harlyn Bay and right round to Booby's Bay are stupendous. Among the tacky modern buildings there are also some beautiful and interesting old ones such as Treyarnon Farm, the Cellars at Onjohn Cove and - though at present it seems to be in a rather sorry state - Harlyn House. It is an area of considerable historical interest: witness the ruined Church and Holy Well of St Constantine and especially the important discoveries at Harlyn Bay of a pair of gold *lunulae* over three thousand years old and a burial ground probably from the Iron Age. The full walk is quite long but not strenuous, and there are several places where refreshments are available, including pubs at Treyarnon and Harlyn, and shops at Constantine Bay and (during the season only) Treyarnon. Part of the route uses a road which can be quite busy during the summer. On the path from Treyarnon to Trevear there are a few awkward stiles. A short section of the coast path at Harlyn may be impassable when the tide is high, but see point 6.

Directions are given from the car park at Treyarnon Bay (grid reference: SW 858740), which is signposted from the B3276 Padstow - Newquay road.

1 Walk back up the road past the tamarisk hedges and attractive "herringbone" walls at the Waterbeach Hotel, and the fine old buildings of Treyarnon Farm. Turn right at the T-junction, and take the public footpath on the left after a few yards. Follow the line of tractor tracks up to the 5-bar wooden gate - which when we did this walk last was tied with a length of barbed wire, therefore hard to open, and rickety, therefore hard to climb. These things are sent to test your qualifications as a walker. Go diagonally over the next field, cutting off the left-hand corner, and cross the slate-topped stile in the tamarisk hedge. Continue in roughly the same line to cross three more stiles. The village on the skyline ahead is St Merryn, and the farm on the left is Trevear. The last section of the path before the road is rather narrow and was rather overgrown when we were there, with a fine crop of sloes on both sides.

2 Turn left on the road, passing Trevear farm buildings and Sunshine Cottage, bearing the date 1790. Continue along the rough, sandy track which ends at a rubbish dump. Go through the metal gate on the left and follow the field edge, with the hedge on your right. When that curves right, bear slightly left across the field to the wooden gate near the houses.

3 Go left along the track into the village of Constantine Bay (*) - mostly modern bungaloid development on this side. Ignore the minor side-turnings, but turn right at the main road, opposite the Constantine Bay Stores.

4 Where this road curves right towards St Merryn, go left, following the sign to Harlyn. *(If you want to make this a very short round walk, take the footpath on the left at the corner, which takes you across the dunes to the coast only about half a mile north of Treyarnon.)* For the longer routes, continue on the road past the golf club house and a line of six wooden

---

CONSTANTINE BAY,
WITH ST CONSTANTINE'S CHURCH AND WELL

Like Constantine on the Helford River, the name of this village was once pronounced "Constenton". Both are named after an early saint. The accounts of St Petroc's life tell how he converted to Christianity the "rich man" Constantine and his huntsmen; he may possibly be the same person as Constantine the Cornish "king and martyr"; he in turn was supposed to have been a descendant of the Roman emperor of that name. Whoever the Cornish Constantine was, he had a holy well in St Merryn parish, whose waters had miraculous powers and attracted pilgrims to bathe their feet, and nearby a Chapel was dedicated to him. This had its own district and regular services; it was rebuilt about 1390 and continued in use for nearly 200 years more. Later it became waterlogged and engulfed by sand, but was never completely buried like St Piran's Oratory at Perranporth and St Enodoc Church; services ceased, although the building continued in use for a while as an almshouse, and parts of the Chapel were taken to other sites, notably the lovely font to St Merryn Church and the tower pinnacles to Little Petherick. The well did disappear beneath the sands, but was found by two local archaeologists in 1911, since when it has been restored and given a protective roof.

chalets. *(For a medium-length walk, take the footpath on the left, signed to Trevose. It runs along the edge of the practice golf course at first, and later between two greens on the main course. Walk with the tamarisk hedge on your right. After a couple of hundred yards, look left to see the ivy-covered ruins of St Constantine's Church on a hillock; St Constantine's Well is down to the right of it, under a modern pitched roof. If you want to take a close look at them, the owners of the golf course tell me they have no objection to your crossing the short course, so long as you accept that you do so at your own risk. Beyond the row of tamarisks, continue with the barbed-wire fence on your left, and cross the stile at the road.*
Here you could go left to Booby's Bay. Although this is not a definitive right of way, in practice it is at present always open to walkers. At Booby's Bay turn left on the coast path to return to Treyarnon.
Alternatively, go straight on along the toll road [don't worry: walkers don't have to pay the toll, unless things have changed since 1990] to Trevose Head. Unfortunately, there is no right of way between this long and rather dreary road - despite some good views from it - and Mother Ivey's Bay, which is tantalisingly close on the right, except by way of Trevose Head, so if you want to visit the headland before returning to Treyarnon I'd recommend you to go down to Booby's Bay and walk to it along the coastal path, returning the same way.)

For the full seven-mile walk via Harlyn, continue along the road. After about half a mile you will pass Harlyn House on your right; in 1990 it was looking very neglected, if not quite "derelict", as Nikolaus Pevsner described it in 1951. One part of it, on the south side, is over 500 years old, and may include a carving taken from St Constantine's Church, but the main building dates from the 18th century. Near its back entrance is an intriguing dovecote which looks like a cross between a miniature water-tower and the Leaning Tower of Pisa; there is a photograph of it in Roger Penhallurick's *The Birds of Cornwall and the Isles of Scilly*, which includes an interesting section on Cornish dovecotes. Not far past Harlyn House the road curves right

5 Just after the bend, take the footpath on the left, signed to Harlyn Bay (*), crossing a stile on the right of a gate. The path runs across a field to another stile, and then you are among more bungalows. Turn right on the gravelled drive.

6 At the road turn left, past the Harlyn Inn, and just before the bridge go left again, following the coast path sign. If the tide's too high for you to proceed, I'm sure you should be able to find a pleasant way to pass a little time at Harlyn; but it is in fact possible for you to use Sandy Lane and The Warrens to get past the obstacle, although these are private roads and not a definitive right of way. The path crosses the beach, and then at a small inlet some steps lead up to a post bearing the acorn sign. Now the path runs along the low cliffs, crossing a couple of stiles, and you look down over several pretty little sandy coves before reaching The Old Fish Cellars. The house is now holiday accommodation, but capstan, anchor and an old rusty winch are reminders of former days; below is a slip, to reach which boats would have had to run a perilous rocky gauntlet. In fact, of course, the pilchards caught in the seine nets would have been landed on the main beach and brought up to the cellars to be salted and piled up in several layers so that their own

HARLYN BAY

"Harlyn" means "beside the pool", and a glance at the OS map will immediately show the reason for the name. In 1900, when foundations for a new house were being dug (necessarily deep in this sandy area), an ancient grave was discovered fifteen feet down; soon Harlyn became a name internationally known, as 2,000 tons of sand were removed and grave after grave was excavated, many of them containing skeletons in a foetal position and with their heads towards the north, together with tools, spindle-whorls, pottery fragments, weapons and jewellery. "One of the richest discoveries of prehistoric remains ever made in the British Isles", claimed the old Ward Lock Guide, although the Cornwall Archaeological Society's Field Guide (1962) refers only to "the few finds". In 1901 a fascinating if somewhat disjointed book, *Harlyn Bay and the Discoveries of its Prehistoric Remains* by the Rev. R. Ashington Bullen ("B.A., F.L.S., F.G.S., F.Z.S., F.R.A.I., Etc.") was published, with later editions recording further discoveries and scholarly deliberations. On the title page of my own copy, a former owner has written, "The burials are estimated to be 5,000 BC." Well, at least one of the contributing scholars does claim them to be Neolithic, but the accepted view now seems to be that they date from about 200 BC. The dig continued for five years, after which the house was duly built, and later a small museum was attached. Since 1974, the exhibits have been at the County Museum (Royal Institution of Cornwall) in Truro, and the site of the burial ground is now occupied by the Harlyn Inn. For a fortnight in August 1976, just before the building of that began, a further dig took place, during which the skeletons of an adult and child were found, crushed by the weight of a wall built above them. It seems likely that they were a sacrificial offering made when the cemetery was first established: evidence of similar practices has been found at Maiden Castle, South Cadbury and other sites in western England. So far as I know, the fullest and most recent account of the finds at Harlyn is in the 1977 issue of the journal of the Cornwall Archaeological Society. Mr Ashington Bullen's book also records many other relics of man's activities in the Harlyn area from prehistoric to Roman times, notably discoveries of cinerary urns and two beautiful gold crescent-shaped ornaments, known as *lunulae*, on the cliffs. These probably date from about 1500 BC and are often described as collars, but may have been head-ornaments. The story is often told of how a labourer digging a pond found them, along with other objects, most of which he threw over the cliff edge; he kept the *lunulae* because they looked useful as knee-protectors, and a bronze axe-head because he thought it might have magical properties. They, too, are now at the County Museum: together with a very similar *lunula* found at St Juliot, they are given pride of place in a case labelled "Cornish Gold", and indeed it seems likely that they were made in Cornwall rather than Ireland as has often been said: see Roger Penhallurick's *Tin in Antiquity.* The Curator, Miss Caroline Dudley, tells me these are the originals, rather than replicas as stated by Jack Ingrey. As recently as 1985 a perfect miniature bronze urn was found hanging out of the side of the low cliff at Harlyn, and this too can now be seen in Truro.

The Fish Cellars, Harlyn Bay

weight forced out much of their oil before they were packed in casks. (For a vivid account of seine fishing and the preparation of pilchards for sale, see *Old Newquay* by S. Teague Husband.) After crossing the stile beyond the house, we were particularly struck by the clarity of the water below, in the oddly-named Onjohn Cove, on that sunny August day: submerged rocks and beds of seaweed were sharply etched against a background of turquoise sand. Raise your eyes from all that, and you have a magnificent view, including, from right to left, Constantine Bay village, Harlyn House, St Merryn village, St Merryn Church, Trevone with its blowhole, Stepper Point crowned with its daymark tower, Pentire Point on the far side of the Camel estuary, Tintagel Head about ten miles beyond that, and the dim outline of Hartland thirty or more miles further still. A comfortable way to observe all this is from the seat placed near the concrete base of what I presume to have been World War 2 coastal defences, overlooking what the maps name as Big Guns Cove. The headland, Cataclews Point (*), is crowned with barrows - hardly surprising on any Cornish headland, and even less so in this particular area, so rich in ancient remains. In the County Museum at Truro is a beautiful early Bronze Age hammerhead made of Cornish "greenstone" which, along with parts of a small pottery vessel and a large burial urn, was found in one of these barrows by "visitors" who "casually opened it up" during the early years of this century. As soon as you round the Point, Mother

Ivey's Bay (*) and the lifeboat station come into view - but unfortunately so, too, does the sewage treatment works that occupies what was once one of Cornwall's most important quarries. The path crosses the road leading down to that, and after the kissing gate it runs beside a large campsite; the attractive beach is somewhat overshadowed by tents and caravans. Follow the coast path signs, through another kissing gate and over a stile, to continue to Trevose Head. The cliff-edge house known as Mother Ivey's Cottage once housed more pilchard cellars. A little way beyond that, the coast path runs further inland, but it is possible, with care, to approach the cliff edge for a better view of the lifeboat house and Merope Rocks. The South West Way continues past more remnants of wartime coastal defences and the coastguard lookout building. It would be hard to find a better position for that: in clear conditions the view extends from Hartland in the east to Cape Cornwall in the west - not far short of a hundred miles in all.

CATACLEWS POINT

"Grey-rock point" is an apt name, because the slate-like rock for which it is famous is blue-grey. Because it is durable and weather-resistant, a lot of it has been used for building, but another of its special qualities is its suitability for carving, and some of the most beautiful ornamental details in North Cornish churches are made from it. One particular workshop seems to have produced many fine objects in "cataclewse" or "cataceuse" stone around the year 1400: Charles Henderson lists "the reredos at St Issey, the tomb at Bodmin, the fonts at St Merryn and Padstow, the stoup at Endellion, the cross at Mawgan, the cross at St Kew, and the carved details at St Merryn".

MOTHER IVEY'S BAY
AND THE PADSTOW LIFEBOAT

An older name for the bay is Polventon, "cove of the fountain or spring". Just who Mother Ivey was nobody knows; one legend is that she was a witch who put a curse on a local field. As mentioned in Walk 3, for many years the Padstow lifeboat was kept at Hawker's Cove, at the mouth of the Camel estuary, but its access to the sea became more and more difficult because of sandbanks, so since 1967 it has been based here. According to Jack Ingrey, the slipway is 240 feet long, and when launched the boat "throws up a spectacular bow wave as it hits the water at some forty knots".

TREVOSE HEAD

The 243-foot-high promontory is named after the nearest farm, "farmstead of the *fos* or dyke". The word "foss" often refers to a moat or drainage channel such as those beside Roman roads like the Fosse Way, but in Cornwall it means a wall or embankment, perhaps for defensive purposes, so in this case the name could allude to the cliff fort that must once have been on Dinas Head. Alternatively, it may have arisen from the fact that there is a bank beside the road leading to the farm.

Next the path descends to the road leading to the lighthouse, which is open to the public, weather permitting, at most times between Easter and the end of September, although there are no fixed opening hours. No charge is made for visits, but contributions are invited. The lighthouse was built in 1846; it is 87 feet tall and on a clear day its beam can be seen 25 miles away.

7 Return along the lighthouse road. A small diversion out to Dinas Head is very worthwhile. Its name is, of course, basically the same as that of Dennis Hill (Walk 3), and indicates that it was fortified in ancient times; the OS map also marks a tumulus on the neck of the headland - an area where, according to Jack Ingrey, many small man-made flint blades can be found. The name of the inlet between Dinas Head and Trevose Head is Stinking Cove; I haven't come across any explanation for this, although Mr Ingrey mentions a time when dead and decaying seaweed had been washed into it by a storm. Continuing south on the coast path takes you past an impressive "round hole" (blowhole or collapsed cave) to compare with Pepper Hole and the Round Hole at Trevone, both on Walk 3. The superb view ahead includes Park Head and, on the skyline, St Eval Church, which was so important a navigational aid that Bristol merchants paid for its tower to be rebuilt. Gradually the cliffs become lower, and it's easy to get out among the rock-pools around Booby's Bay - named, I suppose, from the gannet-like seabird which is, says my dictionary, "absurdly easy to catch". There was a fine crop of sea lavender on the cliffs here in August; unfortunately, there was also a car, doors wide open and pop music blaring from its radio, which led us to wonder whether the original booby might not have been a human one after all. The people who sought permission, before World War 2, to build a housing estate on these cliffs are also relevant to this line of speculation. The whole section of cliffs above Booby's Bay, and also Constantine Island at the southern end, have provided many examples of shaped flints, some from the Palaeolithic period (8000 BC or older), which are quite rare in Cornwall, but most from Neolithic times (about 4500 to 2500 BC); archaeologists have concluded that there was a clifftop industry on Booby's Point and Constantine Island, producing tiny tools from small pebbles. For more detail, see *Cornish Archaeology*, No. 12, 1973. The larger beach that comes next is Constantine Bay, and here it's usually easier to walk across the beach than among the dunes or "towans" behind. (These, incidentally, were within living memory much higher and steeper than they are now: huge quantities of sand were taken away by lorry to spread on the land, so that the marram grass ceased to resist erosion of the dunes by winds and human feet; efforts are now being made to reverse this trend.) Steps on the left side of a cottage take you back to the clifftop, and the coast path rounds the small headland to return you to Treyarnon.

WALK 3
COASTAL FOOTPATH ROUND WALK NO. 3
PADSTOW, TREVONE
AND STEPPER POINT
Just over seven miles.

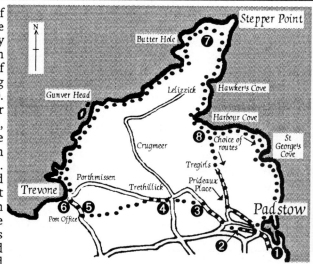

My memories of this walk are coloured by having done it on the hottest day of the scorching summer of 1990. Shade, whether from sun or wind, is a scarce commodity on Stepper Point .... Even in cool and still weather it can't be called an easy walk, because the coast path dips and rises a good many times, and there is one particularly steep climb; but the walk is certainly a rewarding one. The cliffs from Trevone to Stepper Point are dramatic, and once you round the headland the long coastal views are replaced by even finer ones across and up the Camel estuary. Also on the route are Padstow's two most important old buildings, the parish church and Prideaux Place. There are shops and toilets at Trevone. Good bathing beaches are at Trevone and Harbour Cove. The path between Trethillick and Trevone is not very well maintained, could be a little hard to find at one point, and might perhaps be soggy underfoot in normal Cornish weather. An alternative route is mentioned in the directions.

Directions are given from the long-stay car park on the site of the former Padstow (*) railway station, just south of the harbour.

1 Start by walking to the harbour and turn inland past my favourite shop in Padstow (one of my favourites anywhere), the Strand Bookshop, which squeezes more stock into a tiny space than you would believe possible. Turn left at the Market Place and fork right up Lanadwell Street, continuing from there straight up Church Lane (marked Ladywell on the left). Enter the churchyard at the top, and then either visit the church (*) and leave by the north door, or walk around it, leaving the churchyard at the top end on the north side, which brings you to Church Street, signed to "Bird Gardens and Mansion".

PADSTOW

It would be ridiculous for me to try to include the history of Padstow - apart from the occasional snippets to be found among the directions and other boxed notes - in a book small enough for walkers to carry around, so I'll lay myself open to the charge of copping out by simply guiding your research. First, try a visit to the fascinating little museum, where you can buy very cheaply the Rev. B.W.Kinsmen's *A Short History of Padstow*, which justifies its title by compressing it into less than six full pages. The Padstow Official Guide manages it even more briefly. Much more detailed, and therefore much more interesting, is *Padstow and District* by Donald R. Rawe and Jack Ingrey (Lodenek Press, 1984). A useful compromise might be *Padstow Past and Present* by Deborah Goodwin (Tabb House, also 1984), which devotes nearly 20 pages to history and also contains about 30 photographs, old and modern. Out of print now but worth tracking down is *Claude Berry's Padstow, 1895-1925*, a collection of some of his broadcasts and writings plus many old photographs. His *Portrait of Cornwall* , first published in 1963 but reprinted in 1984 with additions by Donald Rawe, includes a good deal about Padstow, and the chapter "Home-Along" is devoted entirely to it. The latest additions to Padstography (don't say there's no such word: there it stands, ready to do useful service) are *Padstow in the Nineteenth Century* by Christine Morton-Rayment (Lodenek), a collection of letters written by her mother, Hannah Nance; Michael Williams's *About Padstow* (Bossiney); and two books of old photographs collected by Malcolm McCarthey (Alan Sutton Publishing).

---

2 Turn left on Church Street. Bear left, ignoring Tregirls Lane, then turn right, passing the entrance to Prideaux Place, on to Trethillick Lane - so my street map calls it, but I didn't see the name displayed.

3 After less than half a mile, opposite some semi-derelict buildings described on the 6-inch map as "Lifeboat House", cross the stile on the left - there is a public footpath sign - and go diagonally right across the field

PADSTOW CHURCH

The town's name means "the holy place *(stow)* of St Petroc"; apparently the a of "P<u>a</u>dstow" crept in during the 14th century when Petroc became confused with Patrick. The church is dedicated to St Petroc, a Welsh missionary who is believed to have built a church on this site in about 518, but there is a story that a church had already been built here by St Gwethenek: hence another early name of the town, Lodenek, a corruption of Lanwethenek, "church-site of Gwethenek". St Petroc, often referred to as Cornwall's most important saint, despite the choice of Piran by the miners, also founded a monastery at Padstow, but its exact site is uncertain. Both church and monastery are said to have been razed to the ground by the Vikings in 981, and this may well have been why the monastic community moved to Bodmin. By about 1100 a new church had been built at Padstow, and this in turn was replaced in the 15th century. The church is large and beautiful, with many interesting features inside, such as the fine medieval font carved from the blue-grey stone quarried at Cataclews Point near Harlyn, several Prideaux tombs, and original wagon roofs which, unusually, survived the Victorian restoration.

beside an electricity-supply pole, over a second stile and straight on to the farm buildings (Trethillick), where there is a third stile.

4 At the road go right then immediately left at the crossroads - a minor road or track leading to Porthmissen, signposted "Trevone 1". At the first field boundary on the left, cross the stile on that side, beside a 5-bar gate. *(Alternatively, you could shorten the walk, omitting Trevone, by continuing along the road; at the far side of Porthmissen farm there is a choice of tracks*

Porthmissen Farm, overlooking Trevone, with Trevose Head on the skyline

enabling you to join the coast path close to Trevone or at Porthmissen Bridge. Both tracks seem to be well-used; neither is a definitive right of way, but like many paths in the area they were accepted for public use by the Prideaux Brune family in 1969.) The path to Trevone goes diagonally to the right, straight on over two more stiles, then beside the field edge (a good view of Trevose Head from here), and over yet another stile. Now you are, or should be, on a track going downhill. Follow it as it curves left and right among farm buildings and turns back into a path going across a field, diagonally to the left. Don't go through the gate, but cross the stile between hedges (walls, they would be called outside Cornwall) on the left of it. Go over the footbridge and curve right, following the stream at first. Beyond the remains of a stile at a broken-down barbed-wire fence - though perhaps both will have been repaired by now - go diagonally left up the slope and cross another stile. This one has a concrete slab in front of it: a footbridge over a stream which was non-existent in August. On the left of the farm gate, go through the kissing gate - a tight squeeze for anyone with a large back-pack.

5 At the road go left if you want to use the general-store-cum-post-office; there are other shops down by the beach, but I suspect those open only during the season. For the walk route itself turn right, down to the main part of Trevone and the beach. Donald Rawe and Jack Ingrey state that the "correct" name of the beach is Permizen or Porthmissen, a name that may mean "acorn port" and could refer to an ancient oak wood long-since overwhelmed by sea and sand.

6 Now join the coast path, going up to the cliffs on the right of the beach and crossing the stile at the top. I don't need to give you directions now: follow the acorn signs..... but don't miss the spectacular Round Hole, or fall down it! You can, however, walk down into it if you have the nerve to use the steep path. Despite the blow-hole's impressive size, it would be quite possible not to notice it if you stick to the cliff edge. Two notable features of the coastline nearby are the double-arched cliff formation known as "Porthmissen Bridge", rather similar to "The Horse" between Porthtowan and Portreath, and the dramatic Longcarrow Cove, whose name could refer to a stag, as with Pencarrow Head near Fowey, or derive from Cornish *garow,* rough. Beyond that are two valleys in quick succession, with a very steep climb out of the second; your reward for the effort is the superb view looking back from the top. The strange stack-like formation you can soon see ahead, Chimney Rock, is at Gunver Head (*goon,* a down or level plain, *veor,* great). 150 years ago there was a small copper mine at Gunver, called at various times Wheal Galway, Trevone Consols and Padstow Consols. (The last two names are an amusing example of the way in which the name of the vast and rich copper mine in Gwennap parish was applied to comparatively tiny enterprises in the hope of attracting wealthy shareholders.) Now Stepper Point comes into view, and on the skyline to the right is Crugmeer, "the great barrow": no ancient burial mound is shown on the OS maps, but the hilltop just south of the hamlet is a very likely site for one or several. The cliff-edge walking is fairly level now for some distance. The cove just past quite a high stile in a wall is called Butter Hole, referring perhaps to casks of butter washed up there, or to what Mark Richards in his leaflet for the South West Way Association calls "the extremely yellow sands"

- but you have to be especially careful when interpreting place names in Cornwall that look like English words: for example, Butter Villa near St Germans is thought to derive from *bod trevely,* which might mean "the house at mill farm". "Pepper Hole", beside an acorn sign a little further on, is almost certainly a reference to the spice, once a commodity valuable enough to interest smugglers; perhaps they stored it in the cave, before or after water pressure created the grim, black blow-hole we now see. There is a Pepper Cove just south of Treyarnon. "Stepper" seems to be another English name. Archaeologists believe that the promontory was fortified in Iron Age times, like The Rumps on the other side of the estuary. The coast path passes the daymark tower, which was being re-pointed by the Royal Navy when we were there, although one big crack looked in need of more drastic treatment. The tower, now owned by Cornish Heritage, was built to help ships negotiate the Doom Bar as they entered the estuary; it was originally painted white. The association that built the daymark also erected capstans on the point to winch in vessels needing help, and tried to reduce the risk of ships being blown on to the Bar by cross-winds by removing a vast amount of rock from the headland; the excavations are marked as "Quarries (disused)" on the OS map, and indeed they were used as quarries during World War 2 for aerodrome building.

7 From the daymark you could keep to the coast path, beside the wall, or cut across the field and go past the coastguard's hut and a World War 2 "pillbox", rejoining the coast path at a stile. The splendid view now stretches from Pentire Point to three or four miles up the Camel estuary (and far beyond that to the high hills of Bodmin Moor), with Brea Hill prominent on the other side of the river and the little crooked spire of St Enodoc Church, now inseparable from the memory of John Betjeman, just to its left. (See Walk 11.) There is a kissing gate above Hawker's Cove, with its row of coastguard cottages and beyond that a row once occupied by the Padstow port pilots. Follow the acorn sign, down to a slip and tiny beach. The Padstow Lifeboat was based at Hawker's Cove from 1827 to 1967, and the boathouse remains; its modern replacement is at the west end of Mother Ivey's Bay. The move was made necessary by accumulating silt in the channel known as The Narrows leading from Hawker's Cove to the sea.

8 There is a stile before the path descends to the large beach at Harbour Cove, and here you have a choice to make:
EITHER for the shorter route, take the inland path across the low dunes and up to Tregirls Farm, now partially converted into holiday accommodation; there you join a road which eventually goes under an arched bridge and past Prideaux Place (*), with its deer park on your left. At Dower House turn left, or delay the left turn till you reach High Street, with tropical-bird cages on the left. Notice, on the right at the end of the street, "Marble Arch", the subject of many a picture postcard. Continue down Cross Street and Market Strand to the harbour and car park.
OR stick to the coast path. You could either stay on the top of the low cliffs or dunes, or if the tide is right cut across the beach before returning to the higher level. At Gun Point - the first headland, almost opposite Brea Hill - are the remains of an Artillery Volunteers Battery dating from 1868, and also World War 2 gun emplacements, all on the site of earlier fortifications. St George's Cove according to the maps has an ancient well, but there is

PRIDEAUX PLACE

The Prideaux family, as their name suggests, were of Norman origin. Their first Cornish home, so far as is known, was Prideaux, just west of the Luxulyan Valley (see *Around the River Fowey,* Walk 12). By 1500 they owned land in and around Padstow. The Manor of Padstow, including what is said to be the oldest deer park in Britain, was then the property of the Priory of Bodmin, but during the 1530s it became clear that monastic lands would soon be appropriated by the Crown, so the Prior granted a 90-year lease of the Manor to his niece and her husband, William Prideaux. In 1545 the Prideaux family purchased the freehold from the Crown. Part of their land was a "Playing Place", an amphitheatre where plays and other entertainments were performed (there is a village called Playing Place south of Truro, and other such sites are often indicated by the Cornish words *Plain an Gwary)*, and it was there that Nicholas Prideaux built his new mansion (Cornish, *plas*) between 1588 and 1592. Its outside appearance has changed little since it was built; inside, succeeding generations added their own contributions, notably when the beautiful staircase, panelling and other fixtures were brought from Stowe, the East Cornwall mansion of the Grenville family, which was demolished in 1739. The fine embossed plaster ceiling in the Great Chamber resembles the famous one in the Long Gallery at Lanhydrock. Donald Rawe and Jack Ingrey in *Padstow and District* give the date of the Prideaux ceiling as 18th century, but the leaflet for visitors to the house says it dates back to approximately 1585 and is therefore some 50 years older than the Lanhydrock ceiling. Even more remarkably, that would make the ceiling three years older than the house! The gardens, in the neo-classical style, were developed mainly during the 18th and 19th centuries. In recent years much has been done to restore the house and outbuildings, and the house has also become something of a Mecca for lovers of opera. It is open for visits during the afternoons at Easter and in the summer, with extended opening hours at Bank Holidays: phone 0841-532411 for current details. If my comments on Prideaux Place have not been enough to convince you you should take a close look, read John Julius Norwich's ecstatic description in *The Architecture of Southern England* ; the adjectives he uses include: glorious (plus "simply glorious"), marvellous (twice), enchantingly (sorry - an adverb!), superb, sensational and tremendous.

no trace of it now; the legend is that St George's horse struck a rock with its hoof, and water gushed forth. At St Saviour's Point there was once a small chapel in which a hermit maintained a beacon light to guide vessels using the harbour. The chapel, like the well, has gone now, and the site is occupied by Padstow's War Memorial and the ancient Chapel Stile. According to Deborah Goodwin (see the note on Padstow), the stile "appears to have been part of the chapel of St Saviour's." The path brings you into Padstow above the North Quay.

WALK 4
CAMEL TRAIL ROUND WALK NO. 1
SAINTS' WAY ROUND WALK NO. 1
LOWER HALWYN, PADSTOW,
LITTLE PETHERICK AND ST ISSEY

About seven miles, including a diversion into Padstow.

This is a beautiful, varied walk, and full of interest, one of the best in the area, and an excellent introduction to the two long-distance footpaths that begin, or end, at Padstow. There are a few snags, naturally: for

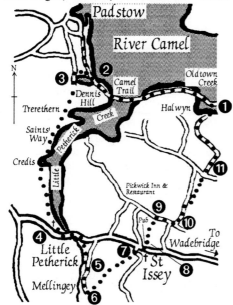

example, it is definitely a route that calls for waterproof (and mudproof) footwear. I would consider it one of the more strenuous walks in this book: there are some steep dips and climbs on this first section of the Saints' Way, and on the final part of the walk. You may have to climb one or two gates on that last section, too, and scale a few awkward stiles. On the other hand, there is an excellent pub at which to relax and fortify yourself, conveniently placed at St Issey, about three-quarters of the way round; St Issey has a shop, too. Also close to the route, just beyond St Issey, is the Pickwick Inn,

quite favourably written up by David Guthrie in *Cornish Pubs*. Padstow, of course, has a good choice of refreshments. A further possibility during the season would be to call at the Mallards Wine Bar at Dennis Cove Leisure Park, about a mile into the walk; and from Easter to the end of October teas are served at Mellingey Mill, which you reach just before turning off the Saints' Way. But even if none of these facilities existed, I would still highly recommend the walk. The scenery at the Padstow end of the Camel Trail is superb; Little Petherick Creek is as lovely and as peaceful as my favourite spots around the Helford and the Fal, which I used to think unrivalled; the rolling farmland passed through by the final third of the walk is scarcely less attractive. "Luxuriant and unspoiled inland Cornwall" is how Betjeman described it in the 1960s, and it doesn't seem to have changed much. Add two ancient churches, a former watermill and various features of special interest to the enthusiast for railway history ..... All that and more, plus the delights of Padstow itself if you choose to include it.

Parking in Padstow during the summer can be both difficult and expensive, so I have selected as the starting point Lower Halwyn, where there is a small car park for the Camel Trail. To drive there from Padstow, take the Wadebridge road as far as Trevance, about a quarter of a mile beyond St Issey; turn left on to a minor road there, signposted to Trevilgus and Tregonce. When you reach a T-junction, turn right, and then first left, signposted to Old Town Cove. From Wadebridge, take the A39, turning right towards Padstow on the A389 at Hal's Grave. Take the first public road on the right, signposted to Trevilgus, Halwyn and Tregonce, and after about a mile turn right again where signed Old Town Cove. If, however, you decide to begin and end at Padstow, start from the long-stay car park at the former railway station and pick up the directions at point 2. Other possibilities would be to park at the village hall in Little Petherick, starting the directions at point 4, or at the Ring O' Bells, St Issey, and read from point 8. Unless you are patronising the pub, you will obviously need to get permission to use its car park.

1 From the car park and picnic area at Little Halwyn (*), go up the steps on to the Camel Trail. Almost exactly opposite at this point is Cant Hill (*).

HALWYN AND OLDTOWN

The first name means "white hall": Halwyn itself was originally a manor house on the west side of the little creek. The OS map marks it as an ancient site and refers to "remains", and Charles Henderson's *Cornish Church Guide* (1925) states that "some ruins of the mediaeval house, columbarium (dovecot), and bridge at Halwyn will repay a visit," but according to Jack Ingrey there is little to see now. Michael Gill's guide to the Saints' Way also mentions a chapel and well of St Madoc at Halwyn, and says that the "ruins can still be seen". The name of the cove, Oldtown, is also that of a farm very close to Halwyn; it could possibly refer to the manor, because the original meaning of "town" was "enclosure", and in Scotland and Ulster the word is still used to refer to a farmstead. In Cornwall there are several small villages with names like Leedstown, Halsetown and Newtown in St Martin. Lizard Town may be a lot larger than those now, but its name presumably goes back to times when that too was little more than a farmstead.

CANT HILL

Jack Ingrey's book on this part of the Camel Footpath has an interesting note suggesting that "Cant" derives from the Latin, *canti*, a corner, and connecting it with the name of a nearby farm, Carlyon, which he says refers to the camp of a Roman Legion. He thus links this place with the Roman fort at Nanstallon (Walk 7). Oliver Padel's authoritative book, *Cornish Place-Name Elements*, however, lends no support to these colourful theories: *cant* apparently derives from Old Cornish, but its meaning is dubious, and whilst "Carlyon" certainly includes the old word for a fort or round, the second syllable comes from the Cornish *leghyon*, flat stones, slabs.

Turn left towards Padstow. The former railway line crosses Oldtown Creek on an embankment, with a bridge to allow the water to flow in and out, and then runs through quite a deep cutting below Ball Hill. Rather than walk through the cutting, however, I recommend you to take the side-path on the left immediately after crossing the embankment at Oldtown Creek. The "view-point" sign is amply justified: the wonderful panorama from the highest point includes, from left to right, the Jubilee Monument on Dennis Hill; Padstow; Stepper Point; Rock, on the other side of the Camel; and Cant Hill, with a glimpse of the windmill at Trevelver Farm just to the left of it. The side-path soon descends back to the Camel Trail. After another cutting you reach the embankment and iron railway bridge spanning the largest of the creeks on the Camel estuary, Petherick (or Little Petherick) Creek. The bridge - still impressive despite comparisons to Meccano sets - was built in 1898. The view towards the sea now features Pentire Point rather than Stepper, and there is a glimpse of Trebetherick beyond Rock. *As soon as you have crossed the bridge you could if the tide is low enough go down the path on the left which follows the foreshore to Sunny Corner; it makes a pleasant diversion. To judge by the maps, at very low water it is possible to continue from this path to Little Petherick, and even to cross back to the east side south of Sea Mills, but for the purposes of this walk I am assuming you will return to the Camel Trail. Donald Rawe and Jack Ingrey say that in the days when Sea Mills was operating as a corn mill, there was a causeway across the mouth of Trerethern Creek and a footbridge across Petherick Creek above Sea Mills; it would seem that the maps are showing a route that vanished long ago. Anthony Hawkey tells me that the County has been asked to reinstate the footbridge across the creek to Sea Mills. Writing in 1936, J.R.A.Hockin referred to the "puzzle" of "how to find the causey across the creek" to the Sea Mills side, and then squelching to Little Petherick through mud "of the richest, plum-cake variety".* Beyond another cutting, below Dennis Hill (*), you reach another small creek almost completely cut off from the river by the railway, Dennis Creek.

DENNIS HILL AND THE JUBILEE MONUMENT

The name derives from the Cornish word *dynas*, a fort: compare Pendennis, Falmouth, which gets its name not from Henry VIII's castle but from much earlier fortifications on the headland. The fort on Dennis Hill was probably once on the site now occupied by the granite obelisk erected in 1887 to mark the 50th year of Queen Victoria's reign. Its height - 50 feet - is presumably symbolic.

---

2 As soon as you get to the far side of that, either continue ahead on the Trail if you want to visit Padstow, returning by the same route, or turn left, crossing a "rustic" wooden stile and going down some rather uneven steps. **IF YOU ARE STARTING THE WALK AT PADSTOW**, begin at the old railway station and continue beside the river, with Dennis Hill, crowned by the Jubilee Monument, ahead. Don't miss the stile on the right just before you reach Dennis Creek: if you cross a small bridge with iron railings you have gone past it. Walk beside what remains of Dennis Creek, now a duck-pond but once the site of a shipyard, and past the shed occupied by the Breakers Windsurf Club.

The North Quay, Padstow harbour.
Behind the fence is Abbey House, the oldest house in the town.

3 Turn left at the road, then left again at the Public Footpath sign, beside which is the Cornish Cross symbol indicating the Saints' Way. The path curves right, and after the gate goes quite steeply uphill, keeping beside the hedge on the right. At the top, a Saints' Way sign points you to the right, over a slate stile, but first it's worth going through the wrought-iron gate to the Jubilee monument, from which the view is spectacular. The signs and stiles on the Padstow-to-Withiel part of the Saints' Way were in good condition when I last walked here, but in view of the way time and vandalism have taken their toll in the past, I'll continue giving directions. Go left to the next stile, then right, gently downhill past a Saints' Way post. On the opposite side of the creek now is Sea Mills (*), with St Issey Church on the hilltop above. Next you go down a steepish and probably muddy path to the head of Trerethern Creek, where there are a stile and a footbridge, then go to the right, up some steps and a steep slope. Keep beside the hedge on the right until you have crossed the stile in it; then continue with the hedge left, and on in the same direction over two more stiles. Next comes a shaly track down to Credis (or Creddis) Creek; the track is very steep, and great care is needed. Two lengths of wooden causeway have been placed across the

28

SEA MILLS

This takes its name from a corn mill dating back at least to the 17th century. It was powered by the tides. Much of the walling survives by which a lagoon over four acres in area was created. At high tide the sluice gates were closed, and the water in the lagoon, which was, of course, much deeper before the silt choked it, powered an undershot waterwheel. A steam engine was used to supplement the tide mill, and Donald Rawe and Jack Ingrey's *Padstow and District* includes a photograph of its chimney being demolished in 1908, by which time the building of the railway bridge had made the mill inaccessible to the larger boats which used to serve it. The same book also gives colourful details about one of the owners of Sea Mills, Samuel T. Tregaskis.

A stile on the Saints' Way overlooking the remains of the tide mill and Little Petherick Creek

marshy area at the head of the creek, but you may still have to cross some sticky patches. On the far side, go slightly right, up a side valley, along a rather muddy path between hedges. This path or track was once used by carts bringing beach-sand up to spread on the fields: most of the soils in Cornwall are acidic, and until it became common to import lime, sand was the usual fertiliser applied as a corrective. Another use for the track may well have been to take copper ore, plus some silver and iron, down to the creek to be loaded on to boats. The OS map indicates that there were mine workings a short way up this valley. Credis Mine produced £9,000-worth of copper during the 1820s, and was again active in 1842 and the 1860s. Other small copper mines were at Trerethern (closed about 1825), and about half a mile north-west of that, near Curchey Cottage. A. K. Hamilton Jenkin thought that this last one could have been the site of Great Trelether Mine, about which there were tales of "fabulous riches underground". (Details from *The Mines and Miners of Cornwall*, Vol. 9) At the end of the track at Credis, a Saints' Way sign directs you diagonally left; walk beside the wall on your right and cross the stile into the creekside copse, St Mary's Woods. From here almost to the main road this pretty woodland path runs along the top of the slope. A sewage farm on the other side slightly spoilt the effect in November, but summer foliage probably hides that completely. Finally the path descends quite steeply, via steps and a stile, into Little Petherick (*).

LITTLE PETHERICK

Like "Padstow", the name derives from that of its patron saint, Petroc, who is thought to have had a preaching-cross and perhaps a cell beside a holy well or "fountain" here. The old name of the village is Nansventen, the spring or fountain in the valley. The illustrated guidebook available in the church tells how, according to John of Tynemouth's account (c.1366), St Petroc "spent much of his time sitting up to his neck in the Little Petherick river reciting the psalter. His food was bread and water, with porridge on Sundays." He is said to have possessed a sheep-skin mantle, and to have kept a pet wolf to guard it. (There is a little more about Petroc in the note about Padstow Church, Walk 3.) Little Petherick Church dates from the 14th century, but at various times suffered such severe neglect that it had to be virtually rebuilt, first in 1740-50, when parts of St Constantine's Church at Constantine Bay (see Walk 2) were incorporated into it, and again about a century later. Soon after that, an enthusiastic vicar had all the inside walls covered with black, red and green stencils. His successor removed all those, and there followed a period of further thoroughgoing restoration, an attempt to re-create the church as it might have been in its earliest days, in Anglo-Catholic style. This work was inspired and guided mainly by Athelstan Riley, who employed the famous architect, Sir Ninian Comper. The antique furnishings and church vestments are now among the richest of any Cornish church. Many visitors find the whole effect very beautiful, and compare it with the interior of Blisland Church, near Bodmin. I agree that both are well worth seeing, and I understand Robin Davidson's feelings when he writes, "Here beside the busy road is an atmosphere of mystery, of quiet care and devotion" (*Cornwall*, Batsford, 1978). Personally, though, I much prefer the simplicity of a church like St Endellion. As Charles Henderson remarks, "filling it with beautiful furniture has concealed the last traces of its antiquity."

---

4 The church is worth a visit; but to continue the walk turn left on the main road, over the bridge. The traffic on the A389 is usually horrendous in the summer, and for me ruins what ought to be a charming village; even out of season the vehicles tend to travel too fast on this narrow stretch, and I very much regret that walkers on the Saints' Way have to go several hundred yards along it. Please take great care. I'm sure you will be relieved on reaching the footpath sign to Mellingey on the right (there is a Saints' Way sign on the other side of the road). Cross the slate stile and walk along the

MELLINGEY

"Mellingey" means "mill-house" (Cornish, *melin-chy*), so it's no surprise to find this pretty hamlet dominated by a former watermill. Nowadays it is A.T.Old & Son's "Willow Workshop", where basket making is carried out. There is a shop where you can buy their products, and round the back a small area where refreshments are served between Easter and the end of October. The original waterwheel was demolished, but Mr Old has replaced it with another, taken from a nearby farm. It was made in 1839 by Oateys of Wadebridge - compare Trewithen Mill, Walks 8 and 9. The original 16-foot wheel was assisted by a steam engine, installed, Mr Old believes, between 1840 and 1849. The waterwheel was powered by a leat taken from the valley to the south east; apparently about 1905 more water-power was added by building a wider leat from the stream in the other valley, to the south; both leats are still there, and being kept in good order. During the season the water from the main leat turns the wheel, and Mr Old hopes to generate power by this means eventually. Above the house is a mill-pool, beside which is the willow plantation that supplies the workshop, and the plan is to open that area to the public from 1991. Altogether, Mellingey seems to me a very pleasant and interesting place to linger awhile, even if you don't need refreshments or willow baskets.

path on the left side of the valley. Keep to the bottom of the slope, over another slate stile, and then walk up to a stile on the right of a farm gate.

5 Turn right on the road, past Mellingey Mill (*), the pretty cottages opposite, which in summer are a riot of floral colour, and Mellingey Smoked Fish and Trout Farm; continue up the road to Higher Mellingey.

6 Leave the Saints' Way now by taking the public footpath signposted opposite, down among ruined farm buildings. Cross the rather high and awkward stile in the hedge and go left, as directed by a yellow waymarker, past another yellow arrow on a post, across circular concrete stepping stones plus a footbridge, and steeply uphill beside a hedge on your left. Head for St Issey (*) Church. The path ends by passing through a farmyard which is used by cows and therefore likely to be very muddy.

7 Turn left at the minor road, then right when you reach the main one - unless you want to visit the Ring O' Bells first, of course; the church, too, calls for your attention, and you could walk through the churchyard instead of using the main road.

8 Immediately past the block of buildings including the pub, and opposite the church, take the footpath signed on the left (or straight ahead on the opposite side of the road if you are coming from the churchyard). It starts at a small gate, and when I was last there I had to duck under a rope at the gateway beyond. Now follow the direction of the yellow arrow to the right, over a stile with a gate, and then go left, crossing the stream by a footbridge just left of a farm gate. Continue roughly in the same line, but a little to the right, to go through (or more likely over) the right-hand farm gate ahead. Now keep straight on beside the hedge on your right as the view across the Camel estuary opens before you, and cross the stile ahead.

ST ISSEY

Like Little Petherick, St Issey is an attractive village spoilt by modern traffic, but somehow not quite so completely dominated by it. Little seems to be known about the saint. He is listed as one of the 24 children of the Welsh King Brychan, and his name along with that of another saint appears again on the south coast at Mevagissey. St Jidgey or "Zanzidgie", the hamlet where the Halfway House pub is, about two miles south east of St Issey, is apparently named after the same person: it is thought that his chapel was originally there. St Issey village was once called "Egloscruk", "the church on the barrow or hillock" - compare Crugmere, Walk 3. The oldest parts of the church are Norman. Church tower building does not seem to have been a very well-developed art in this area: the tower at Little Petherick had a chequered history, and at St Issey the one added in the 15th century was rebuilt about 1680, collapsed in 1869, demolishing much of the rest of the building ..... and in 1989 was surrounded in scaffolding! Perhaps to cast aspersions on the builders would be unfair, since heavy rains apparently caused the problems in 1869, and lightning struck the tower pinnacles in 1895 and 1967. The 1871 rebuilding was done under the supervision of the notorious J.P.St Aubyn; Henderson calls the work "lamentable"; Rawe and Ingrey say "drastic and unfortunate"; Betjeman, usually St Aubyn's chief detractor, presumably had tongue in cheek when he chose the word "robust". All, however, praise the reredos (the screen behind the altar) and other features carved in Catacleuse stone, from the quarries at Cataclews Point (Walk 2), in the 14th or 15th century. Henderson mentions the local belief that these came from the chapel at Halwyn Manor, beside Oldtown Creek.

9 Turn left on the road if you want to call for refreshments at the Pickwick Inn and Restaurant, about a quarter of a mile away; return by the same route. But to continue the walk route, turn right. (In theory, the footpath ahead would cut out a little road walking; when my wife and I last tried it it vanished at a stream, and we had to retrace our steps, but Anthony Hawkey assures me it has now been made "accessible and good".)

10 Take the first left turning, and after about a quarter of a mile go through the farm gate on the right where there is a footpath sign. Walk on in the same direction: not close to the hedge, but heading towards the largish farm shed on the ridge. A grassy bridge takes you over the stream, and then there is a low slate stile with a wooden fence to climb. Walk up the long field ahead, keeping to the left edge, and go through the gate.

11 Go straight on down the minor road signposted to Old Town Creek, which returns you to the car park at Halwyn.

WALK 5
CAMEL TRAIL ROUND WALK NO. 2
WADEBRIDGE, TREGUNNA
AND ST BREOCK

About five miles.
About two miles if St Breock is omitted.
Possible extension of about two miles in Haywood.

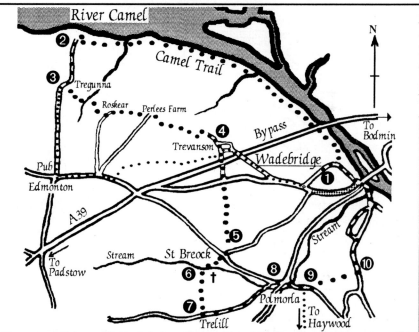

You start this walk by joining the cyclists heading for Padstow on the Camel Trail, and then do what they can't by taking the path over the fields above, which gives you fine views over the river, to the charming little village of St Breock, nestling secretively in its wooded valley, and beyond that the scarcely less attractive one of Polmorla. From there the way back to Wadebridge is through more woodland and open fields. The walk could be greatly shortened by returning to Wadebridge direct from Trevanson (see the start of point 4), or lengthened by up to two miles by using the Forestry Commission path in Haywood (see point 8). You may find the paths muddy and rather overgrown in places; there are a few awkward stiles and gates and one very steep but short climb. Wadebridge, of course, has a good choice of shops, pubs and other places where you can get refreshments, but I didn't notice anywhere else along the way where you could buy food or drink unless you were prepared to make the diversion to the Quarryman at Edmonton described in point 3. Including St Breock on the route involves walking across the new bypass road; those with dogs would certainly need to put them on leads there.

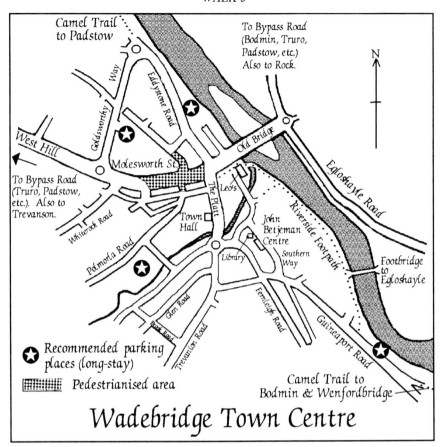

Camel Trail
to Padstow

To Bypass Road
(Bodmin, Truro,
Padstow, etc.)
Also to Rock.

N

Eddystone Road

Goldsworthy Way

West Hill

Molesworth St.

Old Bridge

Egloshayle Road

To Bypass Road
(Truro, Padstow,
etc.). Also to
Trevanson.

Whiterock Road

The Platt

Leo's

Riverside Footpath

Padmora Road

Town
Hall

John
Betjeman
Centre

Library

Southern
Way

Footbridge
to
Egloshayle

Glen Road

Fernleigh Road

Guineaport Road

Trevanion Road

Back Road

⊕ Recommended parking
places (long-stay)

▦ Pedestrianised area

Camel Trail to
Bodmin & Wenfordbridge

Wadebridge Town Centre

Directions begin in Wadebridge at the start of the section of the Camel Trail that heads for Padstow. There is a small pay-and-display car park close by, almost opposite the filling station on Goldsworthy Way, which is part of the new inner bypass created in order to allow Molesworth Street to be pedestrianised. If that is full, you may be able to park on the market site nearby, beside Eddystone Road, except on market days (Monday and Thursday). Failing both of those, try the area suggested for Walk 6.

1 This part of the Camel Trail starts as a surfaced road that runs beside the river. Overlooking the river from the far side is Gonvena House, built about 200 years ago by a branch of the noted Quaker family, the Foxes, who created several famous gardens such as Trebah and Glendurgan overlooking the Helford River. Soon you have a good view back to the "Bridge on Wool"(*). The new bridge carrying the bypass road makes an interesting comparison. As the *North Cornwall Advertiser* put it, it is "*cygnificantly* named Swan Bridge - so called for its slenderness and beauty akin to the bird." Slender it may be, but its weight has been put at 35,000 tonnes. Work on the bypass started in 1991, and it was officially opened by Robert Key, the Minister for Roads, on 8 July 1993. The total cost of the project was over

WADEBRIDGE AND THE BRIDGE ON WOOL

14th-century references to the town call it simply "Wade", from the Old English word for a ford. As the lowest fording-point on the Camel it was the obvious site for a port and market town. At each end of the ford was a chapel: St Michael's on the west side, King's on the east. The magnificent bridge, 320 feet long and with a roadway originally nine feet wide ("the longest, strongest and fairest that the Shire can muster," as Richard Carew wrote in 1602) was built between them in about 1460. In 1538, John Leland wrote of "Wadebridge wher ther was a fery 80 yeres syns and menne sumtyme passing over by horse stoode often in great jeopardie, then one Lovebone, Vicar of Wadebridge, movid with pitie began the bridge and with great paine and studie, good people putting their help thereto finished it with xvij fair and great uniforme arches of stone. One told me that the foundation of certein of th'arches was firste sette on so quick sandy ground that Lovebone almost despaired to performe the bridge ontyl such tyme as he layed pakkes of wolle for fundation." The piers are in fact based on rock, and the picturesque detail at the end of Leland's account has been explained away in various forms - for example, Joan Rendell in *North Cornwall in the Old Days* refers to "one Thomas Lovibond" (though Charles Henderson says his name was John), "who had made his money in the wool trade"; J.R.A.Hockin says the bridge "served the wool trade and the money for it came chiefly from the pious and prosperous west-country clothiers who saved their wool and their souls by buying the necessary indulgences" *(Walking in Cornwall);* and Vicki Ferguson's *River Camel District Driveabout* claims simply that the bridge "was paid for by tolls on wool". Violent scenes on the bridge include a horseback duel in 1543 between George Wolcock and John Tredenick (see the note on St Breock), and the displaying of parts of the body of the young Catholic priest, Cuthbert Mayne, after he had been hanged, drawn and quartered in 1577. The chapels were "profaned and sold for secular purposes by Queen Elizabeth in 1591," says Henderson *(Old Cornish Bridges and Streams);* there is nothing left of them now. In 1847 the bridge was widened by three feet, spoiling its appearance in Henderson's opinion, and further widening was carried out in 1963. The coming of the railway in 1834 gave new life to Wadebridge as a port by enabling such products as granite from the de Lank quarries and china clay to be brought in for shipment; the railway also made it easier for sand, barged to Wadebridge from downriver, to be transported inland for agricultural use. In the long run, however, the railway killed the port by linking it to London (1895): the larger cargo vessels always had problems using it, and now a few pleasure boats are all it sees. The best brief outline I know of the town's development during the 19th and 20th centuries is John Betjeman's in his *Shell Guide* to Cornwall; for a much more detailed picture, see *St Breock and Wadebridge* by James West (Truran, 1991). A small book by Ronnie Hoyle, *Death on the Camel* (1993), is worth seeking out for its account of the Wadebridge "plague" of 1897. The modern summertime plague of the town consisted of huge traffic-jams, but the long-awaited bypass has solved that problem, and the new pedestrianised central area is now a pleasant place to linger in.

Wadebridge from the start of the Camel Trail to Padstow

£8 million.

On the skyline beyond the river (direction about 2 o' clock) is the spire of St Minver Church. Beyond the sewage works the surfaced road becomes a track, and if you had forgotten that this was once a railway line you get a reminder when it passes through the first of several cuttings. Before the second of them is a notice giving details of some of the birds to watch out for on the Camel estuary. Roughly opposite this are two small tributaries, one of them the River Amble, and at the points where they join the Camel embankments have been built to prevent flooding at high tide. Further west, on the same side of the river, one hilltop is crowned with the remains of the old windmill at Trevelver; remnants of white plaster on its walls are evidence that it served as a useful landmark. After some more cuttings you will come to another notice about the birds of the estuary; the small hut beside the water, designed as a hide for birdwatchers - including those confined to wheelchairs - was opened in 1990 by Tony Soper.

2 At Tregunna, where there is a sign giving distances to Wadebridge and Padstow, go up the side path to the right. From the kissing-gate turn left over the bridge, and follow the minor road uphill to Tregunna and Tredale Farms. The road bends left just before the impressive Tregunna farmhouse.

If you want to call at the Quarryman, continue ahead along the road for about half a mile to Edmonton. The name derives from Edmund Hambley who in 1854 had 23 cottages built here for workers at the slate quarries down by the river. After a period when they declined almost to the level of a slum, they have now been transformed into a dozen-or-so holiday cottages attractively grouped around a slate-flagged yard behind the pub.

To proceed from there, either return the same way and pick up the directions at point 3, or take the road eastwards - that is, turn left as you leave the pub and continue ahead over the crossroads. After about a quarter of a mile, where there are a bungalow and a house on the left, the road bends right. Some 100 yards after that, don't miss the narrow gap in the hedge on the left with a wooden stile on the far side. Walk by the fence on your right at first, then cross the fence and hedge by means of two stiles - a fine river view from here. Cross the field, heading slightly downhill through a gap in the next hedge, then continue in the same line over a slate stile. When you reach an electricity-supply pole beside another hedge, walk with the hedge on your left at first, till you cross another stile and continue with the hedge on your right. Go through a metal farm gate and along a cart track which becomes a surfaced lane as you enter the hamlet of Trevanson. At the T-junction turn right, and pick up the directions at point 4.

3 Immediately beyond Tregunna farmhouse, take the track on the left, with a public footpath sign to Trevanson. After the pretty, slate-hung Tredale Cottage, with its attractive views of the river, the path was slightly overgrown in August, and in the valley bottom it's likely to be muddy. In August the stream was easily crossed with the aid of the stepping-stone. Beyond the stile you have to climb very steeply to a second stile and then to the field above that, where you can admire a fine river view as you get your breath back. Go on up over the hill towards the buildings at Roskear, through the second (wooden) gate and continue to the left on a track, passing rusty relics of old farm implements. At the end of the track, go through the five-bar gate and walk diagonally left across the field to the only place I know where there are three stiles together: two wooden ones with a stone one between! Continue in the same direction to a wooden stile in a barbed-wire fence, down the steps and straight on through Perlees farmyard.

Tregunna Farm

Go through the metal gate ahead and down past round silage bins on the left and a pond on the right. *(Note, August 1994: a new stile close to the pond suggests that some changes in the course of the footpath may be under way at Perlees Farm. If so, the revised route will presumably be signposted.)* After the wooden farm gate walk on in the same line, crossing two more wooden stiles as you approach Trevanson Farm. After the stile in the wire fence the path goes down to a stream and then a short way to the right along the bank to an old stone bridge. Cross that and walk beside the hedge on your right, up the hill to the hamlet of Trevanson. Cross the slate-and-concrete stile on the left of the gate and continue ahead among attractively restored old houses and past a post-box.

4 If you now want the shortest route back to Wadebridge, take the minor road which crosses the new bypass on a bridge a short way to the east; this soon joins the old A39 on the edge of the town. It would be a pity, though, to miss the attractive walk through St Breock. For that you have to start by walking across the new bypass road. This can be quite a daunting task, but at least the visibility is quite good in both directions. (A footbridge or at least a central island is needed.) Now follow the road ahead and cross the old A39 - which at least is easier than it used to be. Go over the stile and continue in the same direction. Ignore the gate on the left with two stranded stiles beside it: continue up the field for about another 150 yards and cross the stone stile in the hedge there. Still go on in the same direction over another stile from which there is an impressive 360° panorama. To the right just beyond that you have a good view of the Royal Cornwall Showground (*); ignore the stile leading towards it, and continue ahead to a further stile at the corner of the field. Still go straight on, with the hedge on your right,

---

THE ROYAL CORNWALL SHOW

The Cornwall Agricultural Society was founded late in the 18th century, and a Royal Charter permitting it to hold an annual show was granted in 1827. Until 1960 its venue changed from year to year; since finding a permanent home at Wadebridge it has grown steadily in importance, and each year seems to see both record attendances and record numbers of different types of attraction. It lasts three days and takes place early in June. The 1993 Show is unlikely ever to be forgotten, because it was planned to be extra-special to mark the 200th anniversary of the first Show, but atrocious weather forced the organisers to cancel the third day.

---

and at the bottom of the field go down the slate steps to the road. These need negotiating carefully: not only are they likely to be slippery, but one step is at an awkward angle, and a curved piece of steel which was presumably intended to hold one of the slates in position looks likely to do a far more efficient job as a tripper-up of unwary walkers.

5 Turn right past some pretty, vine-clad cottages, and at the T-junction continue ahead down the steepish lane on the left side of the former rectory. It leads past cottages and through elaborate wrought-iron gates surmounted by an arch to St Breock Church (*), a surprisingly large building for so tiny a village, and obviously it's maintained with loving care. Approaching it from above like this suggests comparisons with Mylor and St Just-in-

St Breock

ST BREOCK

Brioc was Welsh or Irish, and best known for founding a great monastery at what is now the cathedral city of Saint-Brieuc in Brittany. He died about 1530. The Cornish church dedicated to him is old - 13th and 15th centuries - but it was so thoroughly transformed in Victorian times that my immediate impression was that hardly anything old remains inside. Closer inspection, however, reveals a 15th-century font and a 13th-century priest's tomb, and in the so-called Tregagle Aisle (St Michael's Chapel) on the south side is a magnificent slate memorial dated 1598 to the Vyell or Viell family. Nearby is a brass to the Tredennecks or Tredenicks, the parents in Elizabethan costume, and twenty-four children; and among the other memorials one finds mention of the Tregagles or Tregeagles. (The former spelling shows how the name is said.) "Here," as Arthur Mee puts it, "lies the wicked steward who ground the faces of the poor, Jan Tregeagle, steward to Lord Robartes in the 17th century. All Cornwall knows Jan Tregeagle. They say his memory flits about St Breock Downs .... , for he sold his soul to the devil, and his uneasy spirit was doomed to spin ropes of sand and bail out bottomless pools with a leaking limpet shell." The Tregeagle family home was Trevorder, a short way west of Burlawn; a tempting-looking public footpath runs beside it, but not close enough for you to see much of the house, and the path was in poor condition when I tried it. The church suffered floods in 1846, 1949 and 1965; the last was the worst, and the height it reached is shown on a wooden carving near the pulpit. For further information about St Breock church and parish, see James West's book, referred to in the note on Wadebridge.

Roseland; St Breock may not have a creek in the background, but it atones for that with a stream almost literally on its doorstep.

6 The walk continues along the footpath to Trelill (spelt Trelyll on the OS map), which you may have noticed, signposted wrongly as "Trellil" beside one of the cottages, as you walked down to the church. This runs beside the churchyard and crosses a footbridge. For a short cut to this path, joining it just beyond the bridge, turn left on leaving the church by the main (south) door, walk past the tower, leave the churchyard via an iron gate and turn left on the path, uphill. This section of it was rather overgrown when we walked it. Cross the rather awkward stile, step over a low wire fence and go up on the left to cross another wire fence by means of a wooden stile. From here you have quite a close view of the showground, but thick foliage completely hid the church in August. Continue in the same line over the brow of the hill, crossing a field which looked as though it was in use as an airstrip. Head for the rusty gate just left of the house (Trelill); you may have to climb the gate. I'm told there is a stile, but we didn't notice it.

7 Turn left on the tiny and very quiet road which leads prettily down to Polmorla. *(Alternatively, you could continue ahead instead of turning left, along the bridleway through Trelill Farm to join another road near Foundry, where there is indeed a foundry, engaged nowadays mainly in the manufacture of boat keels. The business was started in the 19th century by George Harris, but for the last 60-or-so years has been run by a family aptly* *named Irons. In past years the foundry made waterwheels, devices for moulding concrete blocks, and "sky tips" by which china-clay waste is conveyed to the tops of the so-called mountains. Turn left past the foundry and in about half a mile you will reach Polmorla, where you turn right on the uphill road referred to in line 3 of point 8.)* Interestingly, the name "Polmorla" means "stream or pool at the sea-marsh", thus suggesting that the valley was once tidal as far up as this. (Oliver Padel does, however, suggest that the Cornish word, *morva* , from which it derives, may sometimes have been applied to any marsh.)

8 Turn right at the slightly-less-minor road, past some picture-postcard cottages, and on reaching the "main" road to Wadebridge cross it and take the uphill road opposite, heading for Burlawn, although there is no sign to say so. The road soon dips into an attractive, wooded valley. *Here there is a Forestry Commission path on the right into Haywood which would make a very pleasant diversion if you have time and strength to spare. It continues for about a mile, I believe, and much of it runs quite close to a woodland stream. I have not walked right to the end of it, but a couple who knew it well told me it finally peters out, and walkers have to return by the same route. Anthony Hawkey informs me that hopes of a modification order to make the paths in Haywood definitive rights of way have been dashed by failure to trace the owner(s) of the wood.* The road now crosses a bridge.

9 Just past the bridge, take the path on the left. (There is a footpath sign directing you over a stile, but the path here is overgrown and partly blocked by a fallen tree, so it's better to take the obvious path beside the bridge.) It climbs quite steeply. In the field above, fork right over the brow of the hill and go through the gate. The next stile brings you to a road.

10 Turn left on that. When you reach the new bungalows at Treneague Park, I suggest you turn left through the estate, thus avoiding the heavier traffic. The main road curves right and brings you to the older terraced houses of Glen Road. Turn left at the bottom, and now you're in the centre of Wadebridge, with ample choice of refreshments: for example, three pubs - all well recommended for their food - the Bridge on Wool, the Swan and the Molesworth Arms, are on your direct route along the main streets back to where you started.

WALK 6
CAMEL TRAIL ROUND WALK NO. 3
WADEBRIDGE, POLBROCK
AND BURLAWN
About six miles

After the water-meadows and salt marshes on the south-eastern side of Wade-bridge, the Camel valley narrows and becomes wooded. The return part of this walk takes you up through the woods to the pretty village of Burlawn and then down a cart track with wide views back to Wadebridge. Most of the way, it is an easy walk on well-made tracks, lanes and paths; about half a mile of road walking is involved. The path from Hustyn Mill to Burlawn includes a steep climb and is sometimes rather overgrown; when we tried it in January 1991 the stream was hard to cross, too. You can avoid this path by using a minor road if you prefer; the road is quite steep too, though. The only pubs and shops on this route are in Wadebridge.

The walk begins at Wadebridge: see the town centre map near the start of Walk 5. The most convenient car park is close to the start of the Camel Trail heading south, towards the far end of Guineaport Road. Driving there from the Platt, the short, busy street where the Town Hall is, will take you past the former railway station, now the John Betjeman Centre(*). If you are walking from the centre of town you can use the riverside footpath which starts near the old bridge and Leo's supermarket, passes the new footbridge and ends at Guineaport. (The footbridge is officially named after a well-loved local doctor, Keith Bailey, but popularly known as "Anneka's Bridge" or "Challenge Bridge" in recognition of the contribution made by the TV personality Anneka Rice in getting it built.)

1 Beneath the footbridge that enabled pedestrians to cross the line are gates, on one side of which a notice announces the start of this section of the Camel Trail, once the railway line to Wenfordbridge and Bodmin. Across the river and its flood plain is Egloshayle (*) church, and quite soon after that on the same side there is a view up the side valley running east towards Sladesbridge. The point where the Trail widens, with a seat on the left, was the junction between the Bodmin & Wadebridge Railway and the North

42

THE JOHN BETJEMAN CENTRE

Victorian railway station buildings were a special love of the former Poet Laureate, and it is apt that he should be commemorated here, at the end of the train journey that brought him from London for his childhood holidays at Trebetherick: "Can it really be

> That this same carriage came from Waterloo?
> On Wadebridge station what a breath of sea
> Scented the Camel valley!" *(Summoned by Bells)*

By 1987 the station buildings had fallen into what the Centre's newsletter calls "shameful dereliction"; two years later, Wadebridge Concern for the Aged had completed Phase I of their transformation into a day centre for the elderly with a social and cultural activity centre for the retired. Phase II, consisting mainly of a large Pavilion on the south side, should be well under way by the time this book is published. The original ticket office has become a most attractive John Betjeman Memorabilia Room, already well stocked with interesting exhibits. Visitors can buy books about the poet, and watch a video of TSW's documentary about Betjeman in Cornwall, *First and Last Love.*

EGLOSHAYLE

To add the word "church" is wrong really, because the name means "church on the estuary". St Petroc's dates from the 13th century, but much of it, including the tower, was built two hundred years later; the Vicar then was John Lovybond, who had the Bridge on Wool (the bridge, not the pub!) built, and it is said that materials left over from that went into the church.

Cornwall Railway's line via Delabole to Launceston, and thence to Waterloo (London & South Western Railway). This was in operation from 1895 to 1966. It crossed the Camel on Pendavey Bridge, the iron bridge visible on the left. Soon another bridge carries the Trail over the river. Notice how the river is embanked at the curve, a reminder of the risk of flooding in this area. (Henderson and Coates, in *Old Cornish Bridges and Streams*, tell the story of the cloudburst on Davidstow Moor in 1847 which caused "a wall of water from 12 to 18 feet above the usual level of the river" to sweep down the valley. "A mineral train happened to be in the station at Wenford Bridge, and the driver with great presence of mind drove his engine at full speed down the valley shouting to the people to leave the waterside." At least four bridges up-river were swept away, and "the lowest railway bridge at Pendevy floated gaily down stream and would have done much damage to Wadebridge had not men in boats secured it with ropes and chains." A photograph on page 15 of Fairclough and Wills' book shows the repaired wooden bridge in 1882, five years before it was rebuilt in cast iron. Interestingly, the only bridges to survive the "wall of water" were the oldest ones, at Helland and Wadebridge.) The following stretch of the Trail is a particularly attractive one, with marshes full of flag irises, reeds and Himalayan Balsam in the foreground, and Treraven and Derry's woods up on the right. A lovely valley divides Derry's from Bishop's Wood, and now there are woods on this side of the river too: Gaff and Undertown Woods, through which a "woodland walk" was opened to the public in 1989.

(This is an attractive possible diversion - though quite steep in places - with a map and green waymarkers to guide you. The path emerges from the woods at the road leading north to Bozion Farm and Sladesbridge; turn right on it, then don't join the Camel Trail again but turn sharp right to cross the Trail and river at Polbrock Bridge. Pick up the directions at point 3.)

The Trail itself now is quite close to the river for a stretch, but then the river meanders away and back again as you approach Polbrock ("badger pool") Bridge, an interesting shape as it slopes down to the right and spans both the old railway line and the river. Go up the steps and cross the river bridge.

2 Take the public footpath signposted into the woods on the right at the end of the bridge. Notice the "bat-holes" on the left; it would be interesting to know whether these are natural or man-made. The well-made path runs beside the river at first; keep to the lowest track, even when the main one curves up into the woods. This is a delightful spot, full of pine scents, very peaceful, and free from the danger of stepping under bicycle wheels ..... Eventually you come to the edge of Bishop's Wood, and the track curves left up the side valley I mentioned earlier.

3 At the road, for the shorter and easier way into Burlawn (*), turn right, keeping to the road, and read on from the end of the paragraph in italics.

BURLAWN

Sometimes spelt Burlorne, the name may mean "the house among the elms". The elms are gone, but the village still nestles among trees in its deep valley. John Betjeman in his Shell Guide thinks it "must have been the chief hamlet of the parish before Wadebridge throve." The name of the farm near the centre of the village, Burlorne Eglos, is intriguing because the second word means "church". The celebrated Cornish historian Charles Henderson noted that a chapel and cemetery formerly stood here. Some carved stones, dating probably from the 15th century, had survived for many years in the farmhouse garden, but by the time Henderson paid his visit in 1923 they had been used to fill a gap in a hedge by a tenant who had "considerably placed the carved faces of the stones inwards"! Mr and Mrs Harding of Burlorne Eglos tell me that the smithy at Burlawn was the home of the elder of the two notorious Lightfoot brothers, hanged at Bodmin Gaol in 1840 for the murder of Nevill Norway. Special trains were laid on to carry the spectators - between twenty and twenty-five thousand of them, according to the *West Briton* - and "the town of Bodmin .... presented the appearance of a fair." (See *Life in Cornwall in the Mid-Nineteenth Century,* ed. R. M. Barton, 1971 - pages 69-70; also *Bodmin Gaol* by Alan Brunton - Orchard Publications, 1992.)

The alternative is a footpath, attractive but including one very steep climb, and rather overgrown in places. There is also a stream to cross, and the stepping stones may prove inadequate during wet spells. At the start are a sign, "Hustyn Mill Cottage", and a yellow waymark arrow. The path runs behind the cottage, complete with millstone, then becomes rather narrow, with the stream below. Don't miss the right turning, where there is another

Hustyn Mill

yellow arrow on a post. At the stream, don't take the obvious path ahead but go a little further right, so that you cross a second, smaller stream immediately after the main one. The path climbs a little, a few steps lead up to a waymark post, and there you turn right, going steeply uphill. Towards the top, as you emerge from the trees, tall bracken and willowherb threaten to overwhelm the path, but it was easily walkable in August 1994 when I was last there. Cross the stile in the barbed-wire fence, go straight on across an open field towards the houses, and cross another stile on the right. This stile is just to the left of a newish bungalow and house. Go up the drive, and at the road in Burlawn turn left.

Walk on through the village, passing a well, a pump, the former village smithy (on the right, opposite the council houses) and several attractive old cottages.

4 At the crossroads turn right, following the sign to Wadebridge. Care is needed when walking along this road, which despite its narrowness carries quite a lot of traffic.

5 Where the road bends left, continue ahead on to a "green lane" which later becomes a cart track. The view to the left over Wadebridge and down the Camel includes St Minver Church spire, the Queen Victoria obelisk on the edge of Padstow, and Pentire Point.

6 At the large farm, Treraven, turn right on the track opposite the farmhouse and continue downhill towards the "Bridge on Wool". Go through the wooden gate ahead and walk with the hedge on your left, curving gently left towards the bridge. Another gate brings you to a lane which leads down to the Camel Trail and into Wadebridge.

WALK 7
CAMEL TRAIL ROUND WALK NO.4
POLBROCK, DUNMERE, NANSTALLON
AND A POSSIBLE DIVERSION TO
RUTHERNBRIDGE

About six miles,
plus just over a mile if Ruthernbridge is included.

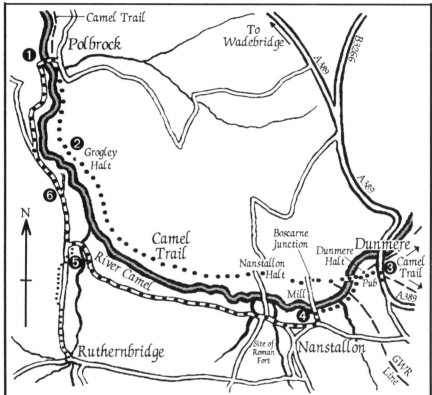

A particularly attractive walk, this. The section of the Camel Trail included has many features of interest to the railway history enthusiast, and the rest of the route has several delightful stretches beside the river and through woodland. The going is easy, with no steep hills to climb and little likelihood of bothersome mud or brambles except on a couple of easily-avoidable sections. Apart from the Camel Trail, most of the walk is on roads, but they carry little traffic. Teas and other refreshments are available at Boscarne and Ruthernbridge; the Borough Arms at Dunmere serves a good range of food and drink; and there is a shop at Nanstallon.

Parking could present problems on this walk. There is space for a few cars on Polbrock Bridge (grid reference: SX 014695), which is where the directions start; alternatively, you could park at Grogley Halt (015685), picking up the directions at point 2 or point 6; or, with permission, at the Borough Arms, Dunmere (point 3); or in Nanstallon (part-way through point 4). Starting at Polbrock mid-morning would give you the chance to have a pub lunch about half way round, and tea at Ruthernbridge if you go that way; an afternoon walk starting at Dunmere or Nanstallon would fit in nicely with tea at Lower Boscarne near the end. To drive to Polbrock Bridge from Wadebridge, take the A389 (Bodmin) road, turning right just beyond Sladesbridge on to a narrow road which climbs steeply past Tredannick Farm and then descends to the wooded valley; turn sharp right at the bottom. For Grogley Halt, continue on this road for about a mile; access to the parking place beside the river (room for about eight cars) is by a short road or track which cuts back quite sharply on the left and is easy to miss. For Nanstallon and Dunmere continue along the A389 instead of turning right, taking the right turning at Mount Charles for Nanstallon.

1 From Polbrock ("badger pool") Bridge descend to the Camel Trail, either via the wooden steps at the north-east end of the bridge, where it spanned the railway line, or by going along the road a little way on the east side of the river (ignore the left turn just past the bridge). Head south on the Trail (that is, go under the bridge if you came down the steps; turn left if you joined the Trail at the entrance gate). The river banks here support a fine crop of Himalayan Balsam, which was a beautiful sight in August; in spring, purple rhododendrons provide the colour. The valley opens out, with watermeadows separating the Camel from the old railway track. This soon passes through a cutting (created in 1886 to avoid a sharp curve in the original line), at the end of which is a picnic table where there was once a siding linking the main line to the Ruthern branch. A few yards further on is the platform at Grogley (*) Halt, opened in 1906. See Fairclough and Wills, page 29, for a photograph of the wooden platform and corrugated iron waiting-shed which preceded the concrete ones.

GROGLEY

This intriguing name is not explained in Oliver Padel's books, but he mentions the Cornish dialect word, *griglan,* heather. Grogley Moor and Great Grogley Downs are clothed with coniferous forest now, but they may well have been heather-clad once.

---

2 *If you are starting the walk at the parking place here, either cross the bridge and turn right on the Camel Trail, or return to the road, turn right and follow the directions from point 6.* The show of Himalayan Balsam in summer is particularly spectacular just beyond Grogley Halt, and a few small islands create a faster flow in the river at the point where another seat has been placed. About a quarter of a mile further on is a third seat, on the left; the large house up on the left nearby is Denby. Beyond the line of pylons that dominates the scene come more watermeadows near Little Denby, and then the village of Nanstallon comes into view on the right, and in the distance the 144-feet high obelisk on a hilltop south of Bodmin. (This was erected in 1857 in memory of a distinguished soldier born in Bodmin, christened Walter Raleigh Gilbert to ensure that everyone would know who his most famous ancestor was. Queen Victoria made him a baronet in recognition of his military achievements in India.)

A little further on, on the left, is Lower Boscarne, where in 1990 Mrs Kath Hamley had recently started serving cream teas and other refreshments in

---

BOSCARNE

The name means "house on the hill", though all three farms called Boscarne are on the lower slopes. Quite close to Boscarne Junction, a mine was opened in 1849, initially to exploit an iron lode (vein), but in the event it produced more copper than iron. By 1852, the workings were down to below 200 feet, and a new adit (drainage shaft) was started near Dunmere, but despite quite promising-looking signs for the future the company went into liquidation in 1853. A little way south there were other silver, lead and copper mines, mostly small enterprises: Thistlemoor Consols at Threewaters Farm; Wheal Atley at Atley Farm; and Bodmin Wheal Mary and Levaddon Mine, near Bodwannick Wood.

---

her attractive orchard overlooking the Trail. She told us she planned to stay open all year till about 6 pm - but if you are depending on getting refreshments there it might be wise to check beforehand by phoning 0208-74291.

The walk continues via kissing gates on both sides of a minor road, with Nanstallon Halt on the far side. Photographs on page 30 of the book by Fairclough and Wills show the waiting shed, level crossing gates and signal box which used to be here; the house near the first kissing gate was provided for the signalman. Soon comes another road crossing, and here there survives a notice, apparently for engine drivers: "STOP Open crossing gates before proceeding." Immediately beyond the minor road (leading on the right to Boscarne Mill, to which there is "no public access") was Boscarne Junction, where the Great Western Railway's line from Bodmin General and Bodmin Road (now called Bodmin Parkway) stations came in from the right to join the Bodmin & Wadebridge Railway's line. This link between Wadebridge and the main Plymouth / London line was opened in 1888. At Boscarne Junction there are several relics of the railway: level crossing gates, rails, buffers and three carriages. Now a former railway-bridge takes you across the river, and you come to Dunmere Junction, where the B&W's branch to Bodmin North station joined the line from Wadebridge to Wenfordbridge. Follow the sign (right) to Bodmin, which brings you to the third platform erected in 1906, Dunmere Halt. ("Dunmere" means "great fort", which is somewhat surprising: the name would seem more apt for Nanstallon.)

If you want to call at the Borough Arms, go up the path on the left before the road bridge. *(If not, turn back at this point, picking up the directions at line 2 of point 3.)* When you reach the road, PLEASE TAKE GREAT CARE: there is no pavement, and the traffic tends to come thick and fast. Turn right, over the bridge, where you will find the pub, a very popular one with a big car park and a menu to match. David Guthrie's *Cornish Pubs* comments, "Things take a little time to happen, eg food, coffee, etc.", but in fact we were served very speedily, perhaps because we were first over the threshold that day. We enjoyed the food, and also the display of old agricultural photographs, saws and other implements on the walls.

3 When you are ready to go on, return over the bridge, down the steps to the Camel trail again and past Dunmere Halt platform. Just beyond the three-way signpost (Poley's Bridge, Bodmin and Wadebridge), take the narrow path on the left, which starts beside some concrete posts. (If this is too nettly for comfort, you could continue on the Trail to the far side of the river bridge, and then turn left over the footbridge and sharp right after that.) Follow the path down to the riverbank. Now comes probably the prettiest section of the walk. The path keeps close to the river at first, passing under the bridge built for the GWR line to Bodmin Road. Beyond the stile you cross a metal footbridge and then a wooden one followed by another stile.

4 Turn left on the track, and at the road turn right. Take the right fork, signed to Nanstallon (*) and Grogley, and bear right at the main road in the village. ("The Village Shop" is a few yards to the left here.) You will pass St Stephen's Church, a chapel of ease for Lanivet parish, and cross a stream which contains trout if the house by the bridge is accurately named. The farm

Railway bridge over the River Camel between Dunmere and Nanstallon

NANSTALLON

Nans or *nant* is the Cornish word for a valley. "Nanstallon" may mean "Tallon's valley", but Oliver Padel thinks it more likely to mean "Valley of the River Alan", which is the original name of the Camel. ("Camel" referred only to the upper section of the river. The tributary now called the Allen was then known as the Layne; its modern name results from a mistake made by the Ordnance Survey in 1888. Even Homer nods.) Just outside the village is Tregear: *gear* is a common form of the Cornish *ker,* a fort or round. Padel mentions five other farms in Cornwall called Tregear plus two called Tregeare; but this one is unique in referring to a *Roman* fort. Its existence has been known for nearly two hundred years, but it was not excavated till 1965-9, and even then little work was done on the western half of it. Even so, we know that it was almost square: modern field boundaries run where the rampart was, except on the east. The Romans loved symmetry: they placed a double-gated entrance at the centre of each side; from each gate a road led to the centre, where the headquarters building was, and another road ran round the perimeter, just inside the single rampart. Roger Penhallurick, in *Tin in Antiquity,* points out that the fort commanded easy inland routes and also overlooked "the most important tin stream in east Cornwall" (that is, the stream running from the Mulberry area to Boscarne, and the Camel valley from there to Cotton Wood; the Bodmin museum has several Bronze Age, Roman and medieval objects recovered from these workings, including two tinners' oak shovels). The fort was apparently occupied for only some twenty years (about AD 60 - 80).

above now is Tregear. Ignore the first right turning, but take the second one, a few yards later. This pretty, usually quiet and mostly level road gives you good views over the Camel valley, though the river itself is glimpsed only occasionally. As you enter Cotton Woods the road climbs gently as far as the house called Poacher's Pocket, but then it descends to the bridge by the long entrance drive to Sunset Farm - another very attractive part of the walk. Next the road curves uphill and crosses the former track of the Ruthern branch of the Bodmin & Wadebridge Railway before reaching a T-junction.

5 *For the diversion to Ruthernbridge(*), you could either turn left at the T-junction or walk along the railway track, which runs on the left side of the road at first and then crosses to the right: a rather narrow path, somewhat overgrown in places, and not shown on the maps as a right of way, but it's obviously used, and makes a pleasant alternative to the road, which can be quite busy. Eventually, however, it rejoins the road, and before long you reach another T-junction; turn right if you want an exceptionally delicious cream tea at a very reasonable price and in a delightful garden setting; turn left to look at Ruthern Bridge. Return the same way, continuing ahead on the road for Polbrock.* To return direct to Polbrock without visiting Ruthernbridge, turn right at the first T-junction. After about a quarter of a mile there is a layby on the right, followed by a track on the same side (presumably the course of the branch line again), leading to the river and Grogley Halt.

6 Continue along the road, which takes you through a pretty, steep-sided

valley; fork right for Polbrock. After an attractive cottage where "wildflower honey" was on sale in August 1990, the road becomes a green tunnel with the river glinting below; then it curves uphill through a coniferous plantation, and the river is still visible between tall, straight trunks; and finally the road descends to Polbrock Bridge.

RUTHERNBRIDGE

The hamlet is named after the stream (Ruthen), whose name possibly means simply "the liquid one", though Henderson and Coates in *Old Cornish Bridges and Streams* suggest it could mean "red river", alluding to mineral pollution from tin streaming, as with Redruth, "ford on the red river". They describe the bridge, with its two slightly pointed arches, as "one of the best preserved" in Cornwall, and date its building around 1450, a period when many fine bridges as well as churches were built.

WALK 8
SAINTS' WAY ROUND WALK NO. 2
ST BREOCK BEACON, TREGUSTICK
AND TREWITHIAN
About five miles

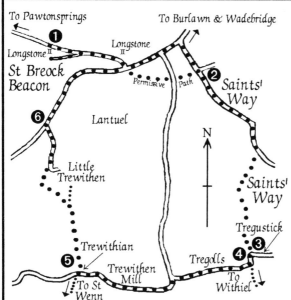

This walk takes you through very remote-feeling and exceptionally beautiful countryside. The view from the longstone on top of St Breock Downs, the highest point on the Saints' Way, is superb; the contrast between the bleak downs and the wooded valley to the south is dramatic; and between the two is a hilly region of woods and fields. Of special historical interest are the Bronze Age menhirs and round barrows on St Breock Downs, which is the highest non-granite area in Cornwall ; there are also attractive old farm buildings and a converted watermill. Much of the walk is on minor roads, but you will need to be prepared for quite deep mud on some of the farm tracks, especially near the woods at Trewollack. About a mile follows the same route as part of Walk 9, and it would be easy to link the two to make one figure-of-8 walk of a little over nine miles, or a round walk of about seven miles, leaving out the road between Tregustick and Trewithian. Further details about these possibilities are given in italics as part of point 3 in the directions for this walk. If you want refreshments you will need to take them with you unless you extend the walk to St Wenn, where the Wenn Manor Hotel is open during the season.

There seem to be few obvious parking places close to this part of the Saints' Way, but there is room for several cars to pull off the road close to the longstone (*) on St Breock Beacon (grid reference: SW 967683), which is signposted from the minor road from Burlawn to Rosenannon. To drive there from Wadebridge, go via Polmorla and Burlawn; from Padstow, drive towards Wadebridge, and where the A389 joins the A39 continue ahead on the minor road to Polmorla and Burlawn, then south-west from there towards Rosenannon.

ST BREOCK DOWNS LONGSTONES

The smaller of the two Bronze Age menhirs on the highest part of St Breock Downs is visible from the road but in a fenced-off field; the larger, called Men Gurta ("stay stone", "stone of waiting") is on rough ground on the summit of St Breock Beacon (216m). "Stay stone" appears to refer to a parish boundary marker; alternatively, as James West suggests in *St Breock and Wadebridge* (Truran, 1991), it could indicate a tribal assembly-point. A few tatty concrete structures, relics of a World War 2 transatlantic radio station, unfortunately detract from what still, I feel, manages to be a magical place. Men Gurta stands nearly fourteen feet high - about four feet of which is buried - and at 16.5 tonnes is the heaviest standing stone in Cornwall. A plaque records details of when it fell and was re-erected. Craig Weatherhill, in *Cornovia*, writes: "Excavation revealed that a layer of white quartz stones had been laid around the menhir, perhaps forming a cairn 4.5m in diameter." According to the 16th-century historian Nicholas Roscarrock, on St Petroc's day, June 4th, every year the priests of the nearby churches dedicated to him (Padstow, Little Petherick and Bodmin) "used to meete at St Brages bicon with theire crosses and baunardes (banners?) at a Sarmon and Collation."

---

1 The walk begins by heading south-east along the Saints' Way. Return from the menhir, past the slate sign to Pawtonsprings (*), and back to the Burlawn-to-Rosenannon road - notice the view of Wadebridge to the left. *PLEASE NOTE: THE PATH ACROSS THE FIELDS AHEAD, THOUGH CLEARLY SIGNPOSTED AS PART OF THE SAINTS' WAY, IS PERMISSIVE ONLY. It may be necessary for you to use the road instead, in which case turn left and take the second turning right. Pick up the directions at point 2.* For the path, go straight on over a wooden stile: one of many on this part of the Way which looked as if they had just been replaced in the late autumn of 1990. Walk diagonally left, as indicated by the arrow, and continue in the same line over two more stiles; the last one is a little to the right of a prominent farm gate. Cross the minor road and continue ahead along a track with a fence on the left and a hedge on the right. After the next stile,

---

PAWTONSPRINGS

This farm is on a part of the Saints' Way which I have left out of the book because it doesn't seem to lend itself to the creation of a round walk, but the name, Pawton, is too significant historically to be passed over without comment. At the time of Domesday Pawton was a huge manor which included eight parishes according to Michael Gill's Saints' Way guidebook; Charles Henderson lists six, "and half Padstow". The site of the manor house was presumably at or near Pawton Farm, some way north of Pawtonsprings. John Betjeman writes that it was "a stronghold of the Saxon Christians set up by King Egbert in 833", and "a Bishop's palace in the middle ages". At the time of the Reformation when Pawton was seized, along with other church properties, it was assessed as the richest manor in Cornwall.

turn right and cross another stile. Ahead now is the Hustyn valley (once the site of a mine, according to the OS map, but I have not been able to find out anything about it), with a glimpse of St Mabyn Church in the distance.

2 Turn right on the road, passing Higher Tregustick. Keep to the road as it bends right, but at the left bend soon afterwards go straight on, following the Saints' Way and Public Footpath signs. In the distance to the left now you can see Bodmin and the Gilbert monument on the hill near it. Cows use the next field, so you may have to cope with mud near the gate ahead. After crossing the stile, walk beside the hedge on the left, cross the next stile, and then go diagonally right. A Saints' Way wooden post has been placed at the hedge-corner; continue in the same line past another Saints' Way marker, down towards the wooded valley. After a third marker-post you go down a pretty but sometimes rather muddy track. Beyond the gate, you may catch a glimpse of the little mine stack at Lanjew, near the top of the hill ahead: see Walk 9; and then the tower of Withiel Church comes into view.

3 At the pretty group of buildings, Tregustick, turn right on the road. Soon there is a tiny waterfall on the right, and the Saints' Way turns left past Blackhay Farm to Withiel. *This would make an attractive short diversion of about half a mile each way, returning here by the same route: the church and village are delightful. Another possibility would be to "slot in" part of Walk 9 at this point, going via Lanjew to St Wenn and north from there to Trewithian, and picking up the directions for this walk at point 5. Two drawbacks to that are that it would mean missing out the attractive road from Tregustick to Trewithian, and you would have to read my directions for Walk 9 in reverse. A third option would be to continue to Trewithian first, and then add in the St Wenn walk by picking up the directions for Walk 9 at point 4, eventually returning to Tregustick via Blackhay Farm and repeating the walk from there to Trewithian before returning to St Breock Downs. (I think I understand all that, and I hope you do too!)*

4 For the five-mile walk, continue ahead along the road, soon passing Tregolls Farm; at the road junction turn left and then immediately right, eventually passing Trewithen Mill and then reaching Trewithian. (For comments and notes on Tregolls, Trewithen and Trewithian, see Walk 9.)

5 Immediately past the buildings at Trewithian, turn up the track on the right, with a sign to "Luxury Holiday Apartments". Ignore the left fork: continue uphill on this wide track, with beautiful valley views to the right. At the top of the slope, where there are a few farm buildings, it is perhaps surprising to find what looks like a public seat - but the reason for it is obvious: the fine view over the head of the valley, with Higher Tregolls (and in this case the name, "ridge farm", seems more apt than at Tregolls, down in the valley) on the upper slopes opposite, Lantuel and Lower Lantuel farms down below, and Little Trewithen further left. Now go through the gate closest to the corrugated-iron shed; the gate had no hinge, so we had to untie and lift it. Walk beside the hedge on the right. The track next runs for a few yards beside the wall on the edge of Trewollack Plantation, and here the mud is, I'm afraid, likely to be deep. Go through the 7-bar metal gate and then follow the rutted tractor-track, curving right at first, which eventually brings you to a metal farm gate close to the buildings of Little Trewithen farm. From here, take the farm's entrance drive, which winds its way up to the road. (The official footpath shown on the OS maps is actually to the right of this drive, but barbed wire would prevent you from getting to the road from that.)

6 Turn right on the road, and after about half a mile turn left to return to the Beacon and the longstone.

The longstone, St Breock Beacon

WALK 9
SAINTS' WAY ROUND WALK NO. 3
WITHIEL AND ST WENN
About four-and-a-half miles.
About six miles if you include Demelza.

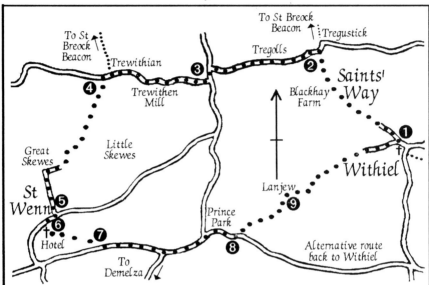

This walk includes only a short stretch of the "official" Saints' Way, but atones for that by visiting one of the churches founded by a Saint who apparently took a slightly different route! The countryside it passes through is nearly all beautiful, unspoilt and peaceful. As well as the two ancient churches, there are several other interesting and attractive buildings: old farms, a forge, a watermill and a Victorian mansion. For those keen on industrial history, there is some evidence of iron mining. You would be well advised to wear waterproof boots and long trousers and take with you a stick and if possible secateurs, in case the path between Lanjew and Withiel is still as badly overgrown as we found it. Don't let this comment put you off the walk: an easy alternative route on quiet roads is suggested in case you need it. There is no shop where you could buy provisions on this walk, but St Wenn has a hotel open during the, season to non-residents for drinks and bar food, both of which we can recommend with confidence.

Directions are given from the village of Withiel, which is about 5 miles south of Wadebridge as the chough flies: grid reference, SW 994654. It is way out in the wilds, far from A roads, and you will need to consult a good map in order to drive to it. Roadside parking somewhere near the church should be easy to find.

56

WITHIEL

The name probably derives from the Cornish word *gwyth*, trees, although some scholars have said that it comes from a personal name. From before the Norman Conquest, Withiel church and manor belonged to Bodmin Priory, and the most famous Prior, Vyvyan, was originally buried here; later his tomb was moved to Bodmin. The church was greatly enlarged in the 15th and 16th centuries, when the tower and south aisle were added, and a little later the small north aisle. The dedication to St Clement, first mentioned in 1478, may have been brought about by a vicar who came from St Clement Danes in London. To me Withiel church seems one of the most attractive in the area dealt with by this book, with its peaceful, sheltered setting, its silvery granite hundred-foot tower covered with a fine crop of lichen (the air must be very pure in these parts), and its beautiful interior, much less drastically restored than most in Cornwall during Victorian times. The white wagon roof, with its carved timbers, is particularly impressive. The village, too, is unusually pretty: there are two imposing houses near the church (one the "old" and the other the "new" rectory, but even the latter is fairly venerable; the old one is said to have been built for Prior Vyvyan about 1520), and the wide main street has many old stone cottages. The one with parts of a cider press outside was a pub, the Old Pig and Whistle, too long ago for anyone I've spoken to to remember. More recently it was a shop. A house between that and the tiny post office is called Forge Cottage; this was actually the blacksmith's house, but the forge itself, in use as such till 20 or 25 years ago, was the single-storey building now part of the post-office cottage. The building opposite was the village school. Withiel may look like the kind of place where nothing ever happens, but every year three events attract many visitors: the Fun Run in April, the Country Fair in August, and especially the Garden Show on the first Saturday in September. Researching this book has taken me to Withiel several times, and I'm inclined to think that I like it best of all the many delightful villages around Padstow and Wadebridge.

1 Follow the Bridleway sign on the right (north) side of Withiel Church (*), and then turn right at the sign, Blackhay Farm, Bridleway and Saints' Way. A bungalow on the right along this path, Copperstones, is (or was, at the time of writing) one of the very few places on the Saints' Way where overnight accommodation may be had (phone: 0208-831970). The green-shaded downhill track just past that is most attractive, with views of a deep valley on the right. Lower down, the track becomes a concreted farm drive. At Blackhay Farm (where there was once an iron mine: see the note about Lanjew), go to the left: not close to the house, but between two outbuildings, past a cowshed, and then turn right down a wide track. It leads to a ford, and even in the dry summer of 1990 it was easy to imagine this as a very muddy spot. Two streams converge here, and are crossed by footbridges.

2 At the road, turn left. This quiet back-road has high hedges on both sides, but you do get occasional glimpses of the delightful countryside all around, particularly when you reach Tregolls ("ridge farm"), with its fine outlook to a park-like landscape. The cowshed here attracts thousands of starlings between late October and February every year: their screeching almost drowned the lowing of the cows when we passed by one late November day. The farmer told us about his mother's nine brothers, born in Rosenannon a couple of miles to the west, every one of whom emigrated in search of jobs as miners. Tregolls, by the way, is another of the very few places close to the central part of the Saints' Way where you can get accommodation; for enquiries, phone 0208-812154.

3 Turn left at the sign to St Wenn, then immediately right towards Trewollack. On the left are woods, and somewhere among them runs a stream, audible but seldom seen until eventually the road crosses it, and then on the left are the lovely gardens of Trewithen Mill (*). Continue up the road to Trewithian Farm, attractively restored about fifteen years ago. The name, by the way, is pronounced "Trewithen", the same as the mill; the *th* is soft, as in *pith*.

TREWITHEN MILL

The house named Trewithen Mill, on the right, was the miller's house; the mill itself was on the left. Its present owner, Mr Rodell, told me that it worked from the 18th century till World War 2. An Oatey millwheel (made, that is, by Oatey & Sons of Wadebridge) about 18 feet in diameter was at the right-hand end of the house, where there is now a new extension. It was in very bad repair when Mr Rodell bought the mill, so he dismantled it, and now plans to rebuild it at the opposite end of the house.

---

4 Turn left on the shady, downhill track just beyond that. After the rickety bridge beside the ford, the track goes gently uphill across open fields, and at the top you have a panorama of rolling hills, farmland and woods. Ahead is Great Skewes; just left of that on the skyline is St Wenn; further left, Little Skewes; behind, St Breock Downs. Go left then right through the group of farm buildings, and this brings you to the farm's entrance drive, which bends left and leads up to St Wenn (*).

5 At the road turn right, past the nicely restored Old Forge, bedecked with horse shoes. Continue past the village school to the church - but if you are in need of refreshments now (and also if you want to borrow the key to the church), walk on a few yards past the main entrance to the churchyard and take the first left turning, over a cattle grid. The drive curves round to the front of the Wenn Manor Hotel, which is open to non-residents for drinks and food.

6 To continue the walk, leave the churchyard by the little wrought-iron gate at the east end. It was somewhat overgrown when we were there, and needed firm persuasion to open. Keep beside the hedge on the right, but where it bends left, cross the rather awkward stile on the right: be careful on the steep steps on the far side. Next go diagonally to the left across the centre of the field, and over the stile at the corner.

7 Turn left on the road - another quiet one which makes pleasant walking. *(At Rostigan you could make a short diversion to Demelza (*) by taking the first turning to the right. There isn't a great deal to see there, but as Betjeman*

ST WENN

A sundial on the south side of the little stumpy tower of St Wenn church bears the words, "Ye know not when". The punning humour of this *memento mori* carries more possible meanings than its author is likely to have intended. For one thing, no-one seems to know anything about Wenn, or Wenna, the saint to whom the church is dedicated; and for another, as Arthur Mee's *Cornwall* puts it, "Certainly few people know Wenn, yet it has something to see" ..... and he goes on to mention "two fine little arcades with granite pillars", and the font, which he says is "probably Norman". Charles Henderson, however, in his *Cornish Church Guide* , calls the font "mock Norman" ("a good fragment of the real Norman font is in the vestry", he adds), and he describes the church as "not very interesting". Betjeman, too, is rather dismissive: St Wenn has suffered more than Withiel at the hands of the restorers. Church and village, however, though less sheltered than Withiel, share with it the atmosphere of peace and remoteness ..... qualities that are becoming increasingly precious.

DEMELZA

The name, made famous by Winston Graham's Poldark saga, has, according to Oliver Padel, something in common with Dunmere (Walk 7), Tintagel, and places outside Cornwall such as Tenby and Tintern: they all begin with a version of the Celtic word *dyn* or *din* , a fort. Demelza is dominated by a hill, on top of which was an Iron Age fort. The OS maps show it clearly enough, on the south side of the hamlet, but it is on private land, and little seems to remain of it now. Winston Graham brought fame to Demelza by choosing the name for his heroine after seeing it on a signpost. He mentions Dr William Pryce's belief, put forward in 1790, that the name means "the honey", or preferably "Thy sweetness".

---

says, it is "remote and haunting", and the walk is pleasant. Return by the same route.) The grandiose Victorian redbrick mansion on the left, Prince Park, was built in 1876 by Joseph Hicks, whose brother founded a brewery at St Austell. It is adorned with many stained-glass windows, often depicting birds. Mr Claude Bennetts, who lives there now, enjoys rebuilding old cars; when we were there, a magnificent 1930s Rolls was on the way back to its former glory. The L-shaped granite house a little further on was Prince Park Farm, restored about three years ago by its present owner, Mr John Brown; the left-hand end was originally a grain store for Demelza Mill, which is signposted to the right but not visible from the road. Just past the old bridge, a new lake has been created by Mr Brown; it is supplied by natural springs which had, we were told, filled it in only a month during a very dry summer. Now the road curves uphill.

8 After a short distance, go through the 6-bar metal gate on the left, just before a hedge, and walk with the hedge on your right. Pass through the gap ahead, and continue beside the hedge as it curves left. Go through the twisty metal gate at the top of the field and along the track, passing to the right of the attractive old farm buildings of Lanjew (*).

LANJEW

The name means "black pool". A "lode" or vein of iron ore runs beneath this farm and Blackhay, which you passed through at the start of the walk, and there were mines at both, though they seem not to have been connected underground. Records show that nearly three thousand tons of haematite were produced at Lanjew between 1857 and 1859, and over four thousand tons at Blackhay during the 1870s. The present owner of Lanjew farm told us that the ore from that mine was taken by wagon to Roche station. His grandfather helped remove the stamps and other machinery early this century.

---

9 Fork left by the farmhouse, and after about thirty yards, where the track curves left, turn right on to a narrow, grassy path. This is likely to be muddy in places, but when we walked it the main problem was that parts of it were quite badly overgrown, mainly with nettles and brambles. Although the OS map shows it as a public footpath, we were told that it is used mainly by horse-riders, and they keep it clear. At that time they were not able to use it, because to do so would have meant crossing a cornfield, but once the corn was harvested the condition of the path should return to normal. We got through eventually, with the aid of a stout stick and a pair of secateurs. I hope you won't have serious problems, but if you do the only practicable alternative is to return past Lanjew farmhouse to the road, turn left on that and after nearly a mile take the first left turning to Withiel. If you do persist with the path, go through the gate and walk beside the hedge on the left. Where that curves left the path continues straight on across the field, but to avoid trampling the corn we kept to the edge on the left side. Watch out for the place where the path continues on the left - another section which was thickly overgrown in August 1990. To the left now you should get occasional glimpses of a small stone ventilation-shaft chimney - the only surface remains, so far as I am aware, of Lanjew Iron Mine. The path eventually reaches a wider, grassy lane (look over the gate to the left for a clear view of the mine stack); turn right on this, and soon it brings you back past the lichen-covered church tower into Withiel. If the conditions are clear enough you should be able to make out the obelisk of the Gilbert monument on a hilltop ahead as you walk along the lane towards the church: see the comments on this in Walk 7, section 2.

The long front gardens of the Post Office and other cottages at Withiel

WALK 10
SAINTS' WAY ROUND WALK NO. 4
WITHIEL, THE TREMORE VALLEY
AND RUTHERNBRIDGE

Nearly five miles.
Could be reduced to about three miles
by omitting Ruthernbridge.

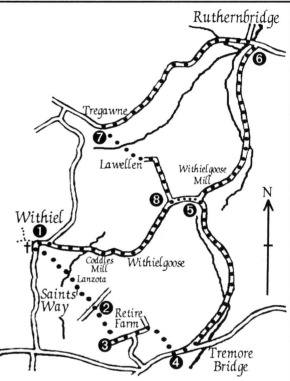

I last walked this route on a glorious December day, when the sun was catching the tops of the trees, casting long shadows and emphasising every slight bump and hollow on the lush-looking valley slopes. Almost all the way I was accompanied by the sounds of rushing streams; apart from the bleatings of some early lambs and various bird-calls, little else disturbed the silence: more than half this walk is on roads, but the sum total of moving traffic on them was three cars and a tractor. Of course, the roads are a bit busier in the summer, and for the three days of the Royal Cornwall Show in June some of them are very busy indeed, but in general I'd be very surprised if you did not come away from this walk with an impression of exceptionally peaceful and beautiful countryside, dotted with attractive and often impressive old stone farm buildings, former watermills and houses, many of them very well restored. In short, this is definitely not to be missed, and I strongly recommend that you include Ruthernbridge if possible. If you will need refreshments en route you would be wise to take them with you, although during the season you might be able to buy provisions at the Ruthern Valley holiday park just before reaching Ruthernbridge, and I have already sung the praises of the cream teas at Boskyger, a few hundred yards further on. Even in dry spells you are likely to have to negotiate several muddy patches. The area is quite hilly, and there are some longish uphill stretches, but nothing very steep. A few stiles are awkward to climb and/or partially blocked: when I last walked this route, in December 1990, no work had yet been done to renew signs or stiles on the part of the Saints' Way involved, but by the time this book is on sale various improvements will probably have been made. In general I'd rate the walk as quite easy. It could be linked with numbers 8 and 9 to create a full day's exploration of this little-known area.

Park in Withiel: see Walk 9, where you will also find comments on the village and its church.

1 Starting at the post office, walk to the church and follow the road curving left (south). After a few yards, follow the Saints' Way and Public Footpath signs on the left. There are steps down on the other side of the hedge; cross the wooden stile and then go diagonally left across the field, but not over the top of the ridge: when you reach a hedge on the left with a Saints' Way wooden post at the near end, keep beside that. Go through the gap ahead and down into the valley, where there is a high stile with a stream on the far side. This area is called Lanzota or Lanzawda by local people, and it is sometimes said to have been where the settlement now called Withiel was originally founded in early medieval times. The name would appear to mean "the site of Zota's church or chapel", and so Zota is presumed to have been a Celtic saint; on the other hand, *lan* in Cornish place-names is often a corruption of *nans*, so "Lanzota" might mean "Zota's valley". Go straight up the hill ahead, and at the top of the slope walk with the hedge on your left. Look back now for a good view of Withiel Church and village. Go through the gate and almost straight on, but curving slightly left to cross a stile with a wooden fence in front of it at the field corner.

2 Cross the lane (muddy in December) and continue ahead over two more stiles. When I did this walk, the first of these stiles was rather overgrown, the second had barbed wire in front of it and both were blocked with wooden structures. Although these were not very difficult barriers to surmount or move aside, I hope that the way has now been cleared. Go diagonally to the right across the corner of the next field to a further stile.

3 Turn left along the lane, which takes you past Retire (*) Farm. If you're weary by now, the Request Bus Stop at the farm may be a welcome sight, but I'm afraid you could be in for a long wait. Keep straight on along a grassy track, but where it curves left cross two stiles on the right; a rather nettly spot when we were there in the summer. Go on down to the bottom left-hand

---

RETIRE

Padel explains the name of the farm and hamlet as "long ford": the first syllable as in <u>Red</u>ruth ("ford at the red river"), and the second as in men<u>hir</u> ("longstone"). The Pathfinder map indicates several tips and shafts in this area: there were small iron mines at Colbiggan and Rosewarrick which amalgamated with Wheal James at Retire to form Withiel United Mines. Hamilton Jenkin mentions that during the 1840s a tramway was built from the Wheal James adit to link with the Bodmin and Wadebridge Railway - presumably the Ruthern branch.

corner, through the gate on the left, and then sharp right to a rickety stile with very steep steps down to the road. Unless these have been made safer by now than when we gingerly scrambled over and down them, you may prefer to go back through the gate and get to the road via the next gate, close by; the owner, Mrs Wendy Simpson, told us she had no objection to walkers using it so long as they close it behind them. As you crossed the field, you may have been surprised by the friendliness of the lambs or sheep in it. Mrs Simpson told us how she reared them "by hand". She shears them herself, and has three home-made spinning-wheels on which she spins her own wool. She also cleans and cures sheepskins and sells them as rugs; enquire at Hillcrest if you are interested.

4 Turn left on the road and then first left opposite The Forge ("the former Withiel smithy", says Michael Gill), leaving the Saints' Way, at the sign to Ruthern Bridge and Grogley. This is a pretty and shady valley road, with deep quarries on the left near the start and a rushing stream to the right. It's worth going a few yards off the road to see it where it tumbles over rocks. Somewhere just beyond the stream were the workings of Wheal Betsy and Penvivian, a small copper mine. Soon the stream crosses to the left beside Tremore Valley Lodge - a likely-looking site for a watermill, perhaps, but most of the milling in these parts was probably done at Withielgoose Mills. Next comes the attractively restored Tremorvah Farm, complete with stables and what the notice describes as "large dogs", whose barks echo down the vale. Tremore Valley Farm is the home of "Wood on Wood Signs": the natural colour-contrasts of different woods are exploited in attractive objects such as beautifully crafted jigsaw puzzles and house-name signs. Even if you don't go in to inspect the items on sale, you are almost sure to see examples of the signs at many local houses. The gentleman who makes them told me there are several small mine shafts on his land and on the other side of the road nearby - perhaps workings of an iron mine called Foxhole.

5 *For the direct route back to Withiel, take the first turning left, and read on in the directions from point 8.* To include Ruthernbridge, continue ahead. Soon you pass Withielgoose Mills (*). The walk down the valley continues as attractive as ever, with the busy stream close to the road, on the right at first, then crossing to the left at Steps, where there is a small weir. As you approach Ruthernbridge you will pass the holiday park I mentioned in the

---

WITHIELGOOSE MILLS

The name means "Withiel woods". Withielgoose itself (which according to Michael Gill's Saints' Way guidebook was a Manor mentioned in the Domesday Book, although in fact the Manor is named there simply as Withiel) is at the top of the hill leading towards Withiel village. The mill, sometimes called Goose Mill or Lower Mill, is first mentioned in documents in 1616, but presumably dates back further than that. It had a long commercial life, not ceasing operations till 1954; the machinery, including the 23-foot overshot waterwheel, was removed in 1962. The size of the wheel, which was nearly four feet wide, and of the building itself - much taller than most Cornish mills - suggests that in its heyday it handled large quantities of grain, although in its latter years there was only one pair of stones.

Withielgoose Mills

introduction, and then across the fields on the left is one of the many lovely groups of farm buildings on this route, West Ruthern Farm. There is a brief note about the stream and the old bridge at Ruthern in Walk 7.

6 Turn left over the bridge, on to a road which is usually rather busier than the others on this route. You soon pass Boskyger - also mentioned in the introduction - and later Great Grogley Farm, complete with millstone, old pump and several staddle stones. These last, otherwise known as steedstones or sailstones, were used to support platforms on which hayricks or granaries were built, to protect them from rats and mice. As you climb the hill, a delightful view of the valley (or "glen", as one of the house names has it) unfolds. According to two small signs, the land on both sides of the road is a "wildlife sanctuary". Bed & Breakfast accommodation was on offer at an attractive modern bungalow with land sweeping down the hillside to the woods and stream; to make enquiries, phone Mr and Mrs Webb on Bodmin 831605. Further on, near Chapel House (Why so called? I tried to find out, but it was deserted) the view is if anything even better. Next comes Tregawne Farm, with its beautifully restored old buildings and its circular duck-pond, and then a pretty cottage called Brooklands.

7 Turn left immediately opposite that, where there is a small parking space. The path runs beside a small stream. Go up the stone steps on the left, over the stile, and walk a few yards left to cross the wooden footbridge over the Ruthen stream - or does it qualify here as a river? It was about eighteen feet wide in December, and flowing very purposefully towards the Camel. Next go left along the track or lane: very muddy that day, but much of the way it was possible to walk along the bank on the left. The deepest and most glutinous mud was close to Lawellen Farm. From there, take the surfaced road, which runs uphill for about a quarter of a mile. Turn right at the T-junction.

8 Walking up this hill was hot work in the summer of 1990, but trees at the top, just past Withielgoose Farm, provided some welcome shade. (I hope you are not too confused by these sudden changes of season. One of the inexhaustible pleasures of walking is provided by such contrasts.) Now the road curves right towards the church, prominent on its ridge. This is a very pretty spot, and Coddles Mill, with its old leat forming a miniature waterfall where the waterwheel once was, and its hens apparently in full command of the road, looked like the perfect rural idyll on that sunny day.

The 16th–century Old Rectory at Withiel

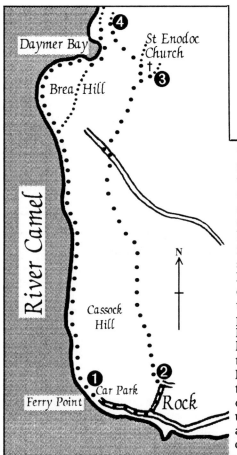

WALK 11
COASTAL FOOTPATH ROUND WALK NO. 4 ROCK AND ST ENODOC CHURCH
About three miles

The original *Around Padstow* included walks only on the western and southern side of the Camel estuary, but for the new edition I have decided to add this one on the other side of the water, because it is so attractive and interesting, and because the ferry service between Padstow and Rock makes it so easily accessible even for those who do not have their own transport. The main point of interest, of course, is St Enodoc Church, now so firmly linked in everybody's mind with the former Poet Laureate, Sir John Betjeman. Another attraction is the view you can get from the top of Brea Hill if you choose to climb up there. Barring that, it is quite an easy walk, with refreshments conveniently available in Rock.

The start-and-end point of this walk is the main car park at Rock (*), which you will find by driving right through the village, to the point where the road ends. This is beside the landing stage normally used by the Padstow ferry; at low tide the ferry discharges its passengers on the beach a little way to the north. (Motorists who want to avoid paying for parking will be likely to find a space beside the road into Rock shortly before it reaches the waterside, especially out of season, and even in August if they arrive fairly early in the morning.)

1 From the car park / ferry point walk along the road until you come to a fairly large hotel on the left that stands back in its own grounds. This is also the point where cross-hatching has been painted across the road. Here turn left up a side road, following the sign to St Enodoc Golf Club (*).

2 Just before the Golf Club entrance turn left, then right at the Public Footpath sign. The narrow, sandy path winds among low dunes. Where

ROCK

The name is a puzzle: few Cornish coastal villages are less rocky. Is Rock rock a well-known local confection, perhaps? Improbable. The answer seems to be that an outcrop known as Black Rock used to project above the sand here, and in "the old days" the ferry from Padstow was called the Black Rock Ferry. Until about 75 years ago Rock remained a rather unpretentious village, but with the creation of the Sailing Club and improvements to the golf course it began to develop rapidly, becoming "exclusive" and attracting famous visitors: George Robey, Jack Buchanan and Kenneth Moore are mentioned by Harry Champion (see the note on the Golf Club). Jack Ingrey in *St Minver, Its Bays and Byways* (Tabb House, 1994) complains about the inflated prices of property which have tended to drive away the "locals", and Mr Champion says "there's not the social life that the real old Cornish community had." It's a picture easily matched, I'm afraid, the length and breadth of Cornwall.

ST ENODOC GOLF CLUB

This is a venerable and prestigious institution, since it was founded more than a century ago and has been graced by many famous visitors, including Edward Duke of Cornwall (elsewhere known as the Prince of Wales), later Edward VIII, who indeed was the Club's president for some eight years. A well-known local character quite often to be seen on the course is Harry Champion, the "jobbing gardener" of Jack Gillespie's book, *Our Cornwall* (Tabb House, 1988). He tells how he would often play with or caddy for such celebrities as Carol Gibbons, Tony Jacklin, David Astor, princes from Thailand and Viscount Clifden of Lanhydrock.

there is a choice of ways, fork right, keeping to the most definite path. This runs beside a fence at first, then takes you through a gap on to the edge of the golf course. From here to St Enodoc Church (*) you need little if anything in the way of directions, because you simply have to follow the white stones. The path they mark out around and across the course is mostly quite wide, and even surfaced in places. Be on your guard for golfers launching small white missiles in your direction. The low hill to your left on the earlier part of this walk is called Cassock Hill, a name that probably derives from the old Cornish word for a mare. After a while the path descends among shrubs to a tarmacked lane; there turn left and then almost immediately right, following the yellow arrow on a post. Next you turn right again, over a footbridge between duck ponds, then sharp left to follow the white waymarkers once more. At this point the little spire of the church comes into view. The path runs beside a stream and a wooded, marshy area, with Brea Hill above. A gravelled path on the right leads up to the churchyard entrance. Just after passing through the lych gate you will see the rather elaborately carved headstone of Sir John Betjeman's grave on your right, beside that of his mother. Inside the church there is a wall plaque commemorating his father, Ernest. Notice also the Norman font and the old wooden chest near it; the remains of a medieval screen; and in the porch a big slate memorial dating from the 17th century, complete with verses and charming if crude portraits of "the father and daughter".

St Enodoc Church from Brea Hill - before the spire was straightened

ST ENODOC CHURCH

This famous little building of Norman origin, surrounded by its square tamarisk-topped ramparts, looks strangely misplaced now amid the dunes, bunkers and greens. In the days of its foundation, however, as the North Chapelry of St Minver parish (the South Chapelry is St Michael's at Porthilly), its site must have been at the head of a small creek. Perhaps, as Jack Ingrey suggests, there was "an ancient trading post" close by. The story of the partial burial of the church beneath the sands is reminiscent of several others along the north coast of Cornwall, notably Lelant, Gwithian, Constantine, and the so-called Oratory as well as the Norman church of Perranzabuloe, just east of Perranporth. By the middle of the 19th century the interior of St Enodoc church was accessible only via a hole in the roof. "On approaching it," stated Murray's Handbook for 1859, "little else is seen than its crooked spire of slate-stone, blackened by the salt breezes and encrusted with yellow lichens. The seats in the interior are worm-eaten, and ornamented with carving so rude that it might be imagined coeval with the ark." Restoration was carried out in 1864 and again nine years later. Medieval spires are fairly unusual in Cornwall (this one dates from the 13th century), and where they were built they often seem to have been intended as navigational aids, either to sailors (as at St Keverne, St Hilary and Rame) or to land travellers in danger of losing their way (as at Cubert). Perhaps the one here served both those purposes. The twist in it, mentioned in the 1859 handbook, was finally (and perhaps regrettably?) straightened out in 1989. Nothing is known about the saint whose name the church bears; indeed, even the name is open to doubt, having taken many forms over the centuries, including Edith, Edye and Nedye. The last version became "Sinking Neddy" or "Sinkininny" in local parlance when the sands around it were so deep that people thought the church was sinking.

BREA HILL

"Brea" (or "Bray", a spelling favoured by many) simply means "hill", and often seems to be applied to the highest hill in a district. This one reaches 209 feet above sea level, and like so many other such places it bears the remains of Bronze Age burial mounds at the top - three of them, in this case. A group of graves (known to archaeologists as "long-cists") constructed of slate slabs has been found on the southern slope of the hill; these apparently date from early Christian times. There is also evidence of Roman settlement in the immediate neighbourhood, and it has been suggested that Brea Hill was at the Camel end of a Roman routeway on high ground that stretched from north Devon via Tintagel, Boscastle and St Endellion.

3 From the church, return down the gravelled path and turn right - that is, continue in the same direction as before. After a few yards bear left towards the water at Daymer Bay and follow more white stones, plus signs directing you to the right.

4 Soon you can take take a sandy path on the left and head back beside a fence towards Brea Hill (*).

Now you have three choices:

(i) If you are feeling very energetic, go up the steps by the footbridge on the left, take the path over the top of Brea Hill and get a fine view of the Camel estuary as your reward. The path continues more-or-less straight ahead down the far side to rejoin the coastal footpath as described in option (iii) below - or you can get down to the beach there.

(ii) Use the beach if the tide is low enough. This is the easiest option, especially if you can walk on the relatively firm sand near low-water mark. After about a mile you will come to the ferry point / car park.

(iii) Start as for option (i), up the steps by the footbridge on the left, but then follow the coastal footpath round the seaward edge of Brea Hill. On the far side of the hill there is a maze of small paths among the dunes just above the beach, but the official coast path runs a little further inland, marked with occasional acorn signs. One section runs along the bottom of a little sheltered valley, often full of butterflies in summer. Where this valley almost comes down to the beach, a half-buried acorn sign directs you up a steepish sandy slope, at the top of which another sign points right. The path then runs quite close to the foreshore, and soon brings you to the car park - once a quarry - where the directions started.

SUNDAY AFTERNOON SPECIALS: SHORTER CIRCULAR WALKS

TEN SUGGESTIONS BASED ON THE MAIN ROUTES

WALK 2

(A) Treyarnon - Trevear - Constantine Bay. (*Under 3 miles.*) (Details are included in Walk 2.)

(B) Treyarnon - Trevear - Booby's Bay. *(Nearly 4 miles.)* (Details are included in Walk 2.)

(C) Trevose car park - toll road and public roads to Harlyn Bay - coast back to Trevose. *(About 4.5 miles.)* (Most of this walk is as described in points 4, 5 and 6 of Walk 2.)

WALK 3

(D) Lellizzick Farm - Butter Hole - Stepper Point - Hawker's Cove. *(Under 2 miles.)* (There is a little roadside parking at Lellizzick, a beautiful old farm in a superb position. Cross the stile on the left, opposite the farm buildings; this permissive path leads to the coast S.W. of Stepper Point. Continue on the coastal footpath to the far side of Hawker's Cove and take the minor road back to Lellizzick.)

(E) Padstow - coast path north to Harbour Cove - return via Tregirls, as described in point 8 of Walk 3. *(About 2.5 miles.)*

WALK 5

(F) Wadebridge - Tregunna - Trevanson. *(About 2 miles.)* (Details are included in Walk 5.)

WALK 7

(G) Grogley Halt - road to Polbrock Bridge - return on Camel Trail. *(About 1.5 miles.)* (See points 6 and 1 in Walk 7.)

(H) Grogley Halt - Nanstallon Halt - road south to rejoin main route just west of Nanstallon. *(Under 4 miles.)*

WALK 10

(I) Withiel and the Tremore valley omitting Ruthernbridge. *(About 3 miles.)* (Details are included in Walk 10.)

WALK 11

(J) This walk needs no shortening in order to qualify!

THE CAMEL TRAIL

The railway line between Padstow and Wadebridge closed in 1967, and after much debate was finally reopened as a footpath-cum-bridleway-cum-cycleway in 1980. The lines linking Wadebridge with Bodmin General and Wenfordbridge continued in use for goods traffic - mainly china clay - till 1983, and then quite soon became part of the Trail, increasing the total length of it to some twenty miles. Two books by Jack Ingrey, *The Camel Footpath from Padstow to Wadebridge* and *The Camel Footpath from Wadebridge to Bodmin and Wenfordbridge* , were published by Lodenek in 1984 and 1989. Since the publication of the original *Around Padstow,* the future of the Bodmin-Wenfordbridge section has been cast in doubt by a plan to restore the railway for transportation of china clay.

THE SAINTS' WAY

This footpath, nearly thirty miles long, was created as part of a community programme in 1985-6 and is maintained by the Cornwall County Council. It runs from Padstow to Fowey; at the southern end it divides into two routes, one passing through Luxulyan and Tywardreath, the other through Golant. Although no one specific route is known to have been used by Celtic saints of the 5th, 6th and 7th centuries travelling between Ireland or Wales and Brittany, the Saints' Way links many of the holy places associated with them. A detailed guide by Michael Gill was published by Quintrell & Company of Wadebridge in 1986, and the County's Countryside Access Department produced a shorter guidebook in 1991. Some circular walks based on the southern end of the Saints' Way are included in *Around the River Fowey.* A cheap but attractive full-colour 12-page leaflet produced in 1991 by Restormel Borough Council (with text by me) details six round walks based on the Saints' Way. It should be available through local Tourist Information Centres.